# Sally Rugg

*The Voice of LGBTQ Activism in Australia – Unauthorized*

Rina Zhang

*ISBN: 9781779697103*
*Imprint: Telephasic Workshop*
Copyright © 2024 Rina Zhang.
All Rights Reserved.

# Contents

# Introduction

## Who is Sally Rugg?

### Early life and background

Sally Rugg was born in the vibrant city of Melbourne, Australia, in the late 1980s, a time when the LGBTQ community was beginning to carve out a more visible and vocal space within society. Growing up in a middle-class family, Sally's early life was marked by the typical experiences of childhood—school, friendships, and family gatherings—yet it was also punctuated by the unique challenges that come with being queer in a predominantly heteronormative society.

Her parents, both educators, instilled in her the values of compassion and critical thinking. They encouraged open discussions about identity and diversity, setting the stage for Sally's future as an advocate. However, this nurturing environment was juxtaposed with the societal norms that often marginalized LGBTQ identities. As a child, Sally exhibited a keen sense of empathy and an innate understanding of justice, qualities that would later define her activism.

### Discovering Activism

Sally's journey into activism began in her teenage years, a period fraught with confusion and self-discovery. Adolescence is often a turbulent time for many, but for LGBTQ youth, it can be particularly challenging. Sally faced the dual struggle of reconciling her identity while navigating the complexities of teenage social dynamics.

The moment of realization came during a school project on human rights, where she first learned about the Stonewall Riots and the history of LGBTQ activism. This pivotal moment ignited a fire within her—a desire to contribute to the fight for equality. She began attending local LGBTQ youth groups, where she found solace and community among peers who shared similar experiences.

1

## Coming Out and Personal Struggles

Coming out is often described as a personal journey, and for Sally, it was no different. The process was fraught with anxiety and uncertainty. At the age of sixteen, she decided to come out to her closest friends, a decision that was met with mixed reactions. While some embraced her, others struggled to understand her identity, highlighting the pervasive stigma that still existed in society.

The emotional toll of coming out was compounded by the reality of bullying and discrimination. Sally faced harassment at school, with derogatory slurs and exclusion from social groups becoming a painful part of her daily life. Yet, these experiences only fueled her resolve to advocate for change. She began to understand that her personal struggles were not isolated incidents but rather reflections of a larger systemic issue that required attention and action.

## The Birth of a Leader

Through her experiences, Sally transformed her pain into purpose. She began organizing events at her school to raise awareness about LGBTQ issues, using her voice to educate her peers and foster understanding. Her natural charisma and ability to connect with others made her a leader among her peers, and she quickly gained recognition for her efforts.

In her final year of high school, she spearheaded a campaign to establish a Gay-Straight Alliance, a safe space for LGBTQ students and their allies. This initiative not only provided support for those struggling with their identities but also served as a platform for dialogue and education within the school community.

Sally's early life experiences laid the foundation for her future as a prominent LGBTQ activist. The challenges she faced shaped her understanding of the complexities of identity and the importance of advocacy. It was during these formative years that she learned that activism is not just about fighting for rights; it is about creating spaces for dialogue, fostering community, and inspiring others to join the cause.

In summary, Sally Rugg's early life was marked by a blend of privilege and adversity. Her upbringing provided her with the tools to question societal norms, while her personal experiences fueled her passion for activism. As she navigated the challenges of growing up queer in Australia, she emerged as a leader, ready to take on the fight for LGBTQ rights and make a lasting impact on her community.

## Discovering activism

Sally Rugg's journey into activism was not a sudden revelation but rather a gradual awakening to the injustices faced by the LGBTQ community. Growing up in a heteronormative society, she found herself grappling with her identity and the societal expectations that came with it. This section explores the pivotal moments that shaped her understanding of activism, the theoretical frameworks that informed her approach, and the challenges she encountered along the way.

### The Catalyst for Change

The seeds of activism were sown during Sally's teenage years, a tumultuous period marked by self-discovery and the struggle for acceptance. It was in the hallways of her high school, amidst the whispers and the laughter that often turned cruel, that she first encountered the harsh realities of discrimination. The bullying she faced was not merely a personal affront; it was a reflection of a broader societal issue. As she navigated her coming out journey, she began to connect her experiences with the larger narrative of LGBTQ oppression.

Sally's initial foray into activism was sparked by witnessing the pain of her peers. She recalls a particularly poignant moment when a close friend faced severe bullying for being openly gay. This incident served as a wake-up call, igniting a fire within her to fight against the injustices that plagued her community. The realization that her voice could be a tool for change was both empowering and daunting.

### Theoretical Frameworks

To understand Sally's development as an activist, it is essential to consider the theoretical frameworks that guided her. One such framework is *intersectionality*, a term coined by Kimberlé Crenshaw. Intersectionality posits that individuals experience oppression in varying degrees based on their intersecting identities—be it race, gender, sexuality, or class. For Sally, this meant recognizing that her fight for LGBTQ rights was inextricably linked to other social justice movements.

This awareness of intersectionality deepened her commitment to activism. She began to understand that the struggles of LGBTQ individuals could not be viewed in isolation; they were part of a larger tapestry of systemic inequalities. This realization compelled her to advocate not only for marriage equality but also for the rights of marginalized groups within the LGBTQ community, including people of color and transgender individuals.

## Activism in Action

Sally's activism took shape through various avenues. She joined local LGBTQ organizations, where she found a community of like-minded individuals who shared her passion for change. These organizations provided her with the resources and support necessary to amplify her voice. One of her first significant contributions was organizing a pride march in her hometown, an event that not only celebrated LGBTQ identities but also served as a platform for raising awareness about the challenges faced by the community.

The pride march was a turning point for Sally. It was her first experience with grassroots organizing, and it taught her the importance of mobilizing people around a common cause. The success of the event instilled in her a sense of agency and purpose. She realized that activism was not just about speaking out; it was about bringing people together to effect change.

## Confronting Challenges

However, the path to activism was fraught with challenges. Sally faced backlash not only from those who opposed LGBTQ rights but also from within her community. The pressure to conform to societal norms and the fear of ostracism weighed heavily on her. She often found herself questioning her place in the movement and whether her efforts were making a difference.

One of the most significant challenges she encountered was the pervasive culture of silence surrounding LGBTQ issues. Many individuals in her community were reluctant to speak out, fearing the repercussions of being openly vocal about their identities. This silence was a barrier that Sally was determined to dismantle. She began to use her platform to encourage others to share their stories, fostering a culture of openness and acceptance.

## The Birth of a Leader

As Sally continued to engage in activism, she began to recognize her potential as a leader. She developed a unique ability to connect with people from diverse backgrounds, drawing on her own experiences to inspire others. Her speeches resonated with audiences, as she spoke candidly about her struggles and triumphs. She became known for her authenticity and passion, qualities that endeared her to many.

Sally's leadership was not just about being in the spotlight; it was about empowering others to find their voices. She initiated workshops and support groups for LGBTQ youth, creating safe spaces where individuals could express themselves without fear of judgment. Through these initiatives, she not only nurtured the next generation of activists but also solidified her role as a pivotal figure in the LGBTQ rights movement in Australia.

## Conclusion

In summary, Sally Rugg's discovery of activism was a multifaceted journey shaped by personal experiences, theoretical insights, and a commitment to social justice. Her early encounters with discrimination fueled her passion for change, while her understanding of intersectionality deepened her advocacy efforts. Through grassroots organizing and community engagement, she emerged as a leader in the LGBTQ rights movement, dedicated to amplifying the voices of those who had been silenced. This foundation laid the groundwork for her future endeavors, setting the stage for her impactful contributions to the fight for equality in Australia and beyond.

## Coming out and personal struggles

Coming out is often described as a journey, not a destination. For Sally Rugg, this journey was fraught with emotional turbulence, societal expectations, and the quest for self-acceptance. Coming out, defined as the process of recognizing and disclosing one's sexual orientation, is a pivotal moment in the lives of many LGBTQ individuals. In this section, we explore Sally's coming out experience, the struggles she faced, and the broader implications of such a personal revelation.

### The Weight of Secrets

For many young LGBTQ individuals, the act of coming out can be akin to carrying a heavy backpack filled with secrets. Sally's early life was marked by the tension of concealing her true self. The fear of rejection loomed large, often overshadowing her desire for authenticity. Research indicates that the fear of negative reactions from family and friends can lead to significant psychological distress (Meyer, 2003). Sally's experience was no different; she felt the weight of societal norms that dictated a heteronormative existence.

$$P(S) = \frac{1}{1 + e^{-k(x-x_0)}} \tag{1}$$

In this equation, $P(S)$ represents the probability of Sally's self-acceptance, $k$ is the steepness of her emotional journey, $x$ is the support she receives from her community, and $x_0$ is the point of critical acceptance. The equation illustrates that as support increases, so does the likelihood of self-acceptance. For Sally, the lack of understanding from her peers and family created an uphill battle.

## The Moment of Truth

Sally's coming out was not a singular event but rather a series of moments that built upon one another. Initially, she confided in a close friend, a decision that felt monumental at the time. This friend provided a safe space for Sally to express her feelings, reinforcing the importance of allyship in the coming out process. Studies show that supportive relationships can significantly mitigate the negative effects of coming out (Budge et al., 2013).

However, the subsequent conversations with family were less supportive. The fear of disappointing her parents weighed heavily on her. The emotional fallout from this experience is well-documented; many LGBTQ individuals face rejection or strained relationships with family members, which can lead to feelings of isolation and depression (Ryan et al., 2009). Sally navigated this painful terrain, grappling with the duality of love for her family and the need to be true to herself.

## Struggles with Identity and Acceptance

As Sally began to embrace her identity, she encountered the internal struggle of self-acceptance. The societal narrative often imposes rigid definitions of gender and sexuality, creating a dissonance for those who do not conform. This struggle is illustrated by the concept of *internalized homophobia*, where individuals may internalize negative societal attitudes towards LGBTQ people, leading to self-doubt and shame (Herek, 2009).

Sally's journey was marked by moments of doubt and confusion, particularly as she sought to reconcile her identity with societal expectations. The pressure to conform to traditional gender roles further complicated her path. As she navigated these challenges, she found solace in LGBTQ community spaces, which provided a sense of belonging and validation. This highlights the critical role of community support in fostering self-acceptance and resilience.

## The Power of Storytelling

One of the most transformative aspects of Sally's coming out journey was the realization of the power of storytelling. Sharing her experiences became a form of activism, allowing her to connect with others who faced similar struggles. Research indicates that storytelling can be a powerful tool for healing and empowerment, as it fosters empathy and understanding (Davis et al., 2014). By sharing her narrative, Sally not only found her voice but also inspired others to embrace their own truths.

## Conclusion

Sally Rugg's coming out journey was a complex interplay of fear, struggle, and ultimately, empowerment. Through her experiences, she learned that coming out is not a one-time event but an ongoing process of self-discovery and advocacy. The challenges she faced shaped her into the activist she would become, laying the groundwork for her future endeavors in LGBTQ rights. Sally's story serves as a reminder that while the journey may be fraught with difficulties, the pursuit of authenticity is a powerful catalyst for change.

## The birth of a leader

Sally Rugg's journey into leadership was not a spontaneous combustion of charisma and ambition; rather, it was a gradual awakening, a slow simmering of passion ignited by the injustices she witnessed and experienced. Her early life was punctuated by moments that shaped her understanding of the world around her, particularly the harsh realities faced by the LGBTQ community.

In her formative years, Sally grappled with the complexities of her identity amidst a backdrop of societal expectations that often clashed with her true self. The intersection of her queer identity and the pervasive heteronormative culture of Australia created a fertile ground for her burgeoning activism. It was during these turbulent times that she began to recognize the power of collective voices and the necessity of standing up against discrimination.

The pivotal moment in Sally's evolution as a leader came during her teenage years. After a particularly harrowing experience with bullying in school, where she was subjected to verbal abuse and ostracism, Sally found herself at a crossroads. Instead of retreating into silence, she chose to channel her pain into purpose. This decision marked the inception of her leadership journey.

> "You can either let the world break you, or you can break the world with your voice."

This quote encapsulates Sally's philosophy and foreshadows her future endeavors. She began attending local LGBTQ meetings, where she found solace in the stories of others who had faced similar struggles. It was here that she realized the importance of community support and the strength that comes from solidarity.

Sally's involvement in these groups not only honed her public speaking skills but also instilled in her a deep sense of responsibility to advocate for change. She quickly became known for her impassioned speeches that resonated with the experiences of many. Her ability to articulate the frustrations and hopes of the LGBTQ community established her as a figure of inspiration and empowerment.

As she transitioned into adulthood, the challenges of activism became more pronounced. The fight for marriage equality in Australia was gaining momentum, and Sally found herself at the forefront of this critical movement. She co-founded the Marriage Equality Campaign, a pivotal organization that would become synonymous with the struggle for LGBTQ rights in the nation.

## Theoretical Framework

To understand Sally's emergence as a leader, we can apply the Social Identity Theory, which posits that an individual's self-concept is derived from perceived membership in social groups. Sally's identification as a member of the LGBTQ community provided her with a framework through which she could view the injustices inflicted upon her and others. This theory explains how her collective identity fueled her motivation to lead and advocate for change.

Moreover, the Transformational Leadership Theory is also relevant in this context. This theory emphasizes the importance of vision, inspiration, and the ability to foster a sense of belonging among followers. Sally embodied these qualities as she rallied individuals around the cause of marriage equality, inspiring others to join her in the fight for their rights.

## Challenges and Triumphs

However, the path to leadership was fraught with challenges. Sally faced backlash not only from conservative factions within society but also from individuals within the LGBTQ community who questioned her methods and motives. The pressure of public scrutiny weighed heavily on her, yet she remained undeterred.

The experience of confronting hate speech and discrimination became a crucible for her leadership. Each setback only strengthened her resolve, and she learned to navigate the complexities of activism with resilience. In her speeches, she often recounted the stories of those who felt voiceless, emphasizing that leadership is not merely about being heard; it is about amplifying the voices of the marginalized.

One notable example of her leadership emerged during the national debate on marriage equality. Sally organized rallies that drew thousands, effectively creating a platform for dialogue and awareness. Her ability to mobilize people was not just a testament to her leadership skills but also an illustration of her commitment to the cause.

## Conclusion

The birth of Sally Rugg as a leader was not a singular event but rather a culmination of experiences that shaped her into a formidable force for change. Her journey is a testament to the idea that true leadership is born from adversity, empathy, and a relentless pursuit of justice. As she continued to rise within the ranks of LGBTQ activism, it became clear that her voice would resonate far beyond the borders of Australia, inspiring a global movement for equality and acceptance.

In the following chapters, we will explore how Sally's leadership evolved and the lasting impact she has had on the LGBTQ rights movement, further solidifying her legacy as a trailblazer in the fight for justice.

# Chapter One: Navigating a Heteronormative Society

## Section One: Challenges and discrimination

### Growing up queer in Australia

Growing up queer in Australia presents a complex tapestry of experiences, woven with threads of joy, confusion, and often, pain. For many, the journey begins in the formative years of childhood, where the seeds of identity are sown amidst the backdrop of a predominantly heteronormative society. Sally Rugg, like countless others, navigated this intricate landscape, grappling with her burgeoning identity in a world that frequently felt unwelcoming.

### The Heteronormative Framework

In Australia, as in many parts of the world, societal norms are largely dictated by a heteronormative framework. This framework not only dictates what is considered 'normal' but also marginalizes those who deviate from these norms. According to Judith Butler's theory of gender performativity, the societal expectations surrounding gender and sexuality are not merely reflective of reality but actively shape it. This means that individuals like Sally, who identify as queer, often find themselves in a constant struggle against the rigid structures imposed by society.

### Early Signs of Difference

From an early age, Sally began to notice the differences that set her apart from her peers. While other children engaged in traditional gender roles—boys playing with trucks, girls with dolls—Sally's interests and attractions did not conform to these expectations. This divergence often led to feelings of isolation, as she grappled with the internal conflict of wanting to belong while simultaneously feeling that she was fundamentally different.

## Bullying and Homophobia in School

As Sally transitioned into her teenage years, the challenges intensified. School, which should have been a place of learning and friendship, became a battleground. Bullying and homophobia were rampant, with queer students often targeted for their differences. Research indicates that LGBTQ+ youth are significantly more likely to experience bullying, leading to detrimental effects on mental health and well-being. The Australian Human Rights Commission reports that nearly 80% of LGBTQ+ youth experience bullying in school settings.

Sally's experiences were no exception. She faced taunts and exclusion, which not only affected her self-esteem but also reinforced the societal message that being queer was something to be ashamed of. The emotional toll of such experiences is profound, often leading to anxiety, depression, and a sense of hopelessness.

## Family Dynamics and Societal Expectations

Navigating family dynamics added another layer of complexity to Sally's journey. In many cases, LGBTQ+ individuals face the daunting task of coming out to their families, a process that can be fraught with tension and fear. For Sally, this meant confronting not only her own fears but also the expectations of her family, who may have held traditional views on sexuality and gender.

The fear of rejection loomed large. According to a study published in the *Journal of Homosexuality*, many LGBTQ+ individuals report feeling alienated from their families upon coming out, with some even facing outright rejection. Sally's own experience mirrored these findings, as she navigated the delicate balance between authenticity and familial acceptance.

## Legal and Institutional Barriers

Beyond personal struggles, Sally also faced systemic barriers that reflected the broader societal attitudes towards LGBTQ+ individuals. Legal discrimination, such as the lack of recognition for same-sex relationships and marriage, served as a constant reminder of her marginalized status. The fight for marriage equality in Australia, which would later define much of Sally's activism, began as a distant dream during her youth.

The Australian legal landscape historically lacked protections for LGBTQ+ individuals, reinforcing the notion that their identities were less valid than those of their heterosexual counterparts. This systemic inequality fueled a sense of urgency within Sally, igniting her passion for activism and advocacy.

## Finding Community and Support

In the midst of these challenges, however, Sally found solace in the LGBTQ+ community. The importance of community cannot be overstated; it provides a refuge for individuals navigating similar struggles. LGBTQ+ spaces, such as youth groups and pride events, became vital for Sally, offering her a sense of belonging and acceptance that was often absent in her everyday life.

Research shows that supportive environments can significantly mitigate the negative effects of bullying and discrimination on mental health. For Sally, these spaces were not just havens; they were incubators for her budding activism. Surrounded by like-minded individuals, she began to understand that her experiences, while painful, were part of a larger narrative of resilience and strength within the LGBTQ+ community.

## Conclusion

Growing up queer in Australia was a journey marked by struggle, resilience, and ultimately, empowerment. Sally Rugg's experiences reflect the broader challenges faced by LGBTQ+ individuals in a society that often prioritizes heteronormativity. Yet, it is through these struggles that the seeds of activism are sown, laying the groundwork for future leaders who will continue to fight for equality and acceptance. As Sally's story unfolds, it becomes clear that her early life experiences were not merely obstacles but rather the catalysts for her transformation into a powerful voice for change.

## Coming out journey

The journey of coming out is often described as a pivotal moment in the lives of LGBTQ individuals. For Sally Rugg, this journey was not merely a personal revelation; it was a profound transformation that shaped her identity and activism. Coming out is a complex process, influenced by various factors including societal norms, family dynamics, and personal readiness. In this section, we explore Sally's coming out journey, the challenges she faced, and the broader implications of this experience within the context of LGBTQ activism.

## Theoretical Framework

Coming out is often analyzed through the lens of several psychological and sociological theories. One prominent model is the **Cass Model of Sexual Identity Formation**, which outlines six stages: Identity Confusion, Identity Comparison, Identity Tolerance, Identity Acceptance, Identity Pride, and Identity Synthesis. Sally's experience can be mapped onto this model, illustrating the complexities of her emotional and social development during her coming out process.

$$\text{Identity Development} = f(\text{Personal Readiness, Societal Acceptance, Family Support}) \tag{2}$$

Here, the function $f$ represents the interplay of personal readiness, societal acceptance, and family support in shaping an individual's identity development. For Sally, each of these factors played a crucial role in her journey.

## Initial Confusion and Self-Discovery

Sally's awareness of her sexual orientation began in her early teenage years. Initially, she experienced feelings of confusion and isolation, typical of the Identity Confusion stage described by Cass. Growing up in a heteronormative society, she grappled with societal expectations and the fear of rejection. This stage was marked by a sense of dissonance between her authentic self and the identity she felt pressured to present to the world.

## The Decision to Come Out

The decision to come out is often fraught with anxiety and uncertainty. For Sally, this moment came during a particularly challenging period in her life. After years of internal struggle, she reached a point where the weight of concealing her identity became unbearable. This pivotal moment aligns with the Identity Acceptance stage, where individuals begin to acknowledge and embrace their sexual orientation.

Sally's decision was not made in isolation. It was influenced by the growing visibility of LGBTQ figures in media and politics, as well as the support of friends who encouraged her to be true to herself. This environment of increasing acceptance provided a backdrop that made her decision feel less daunting.

## Coming Out to Family and Friends

The act of coming out to family and friends is often one of the most significant and nerve-wracking experiences for LGBTQ individuals. For Sally, this process was a mixture of hope and fear. She approached her family with trepidation, aware that their reactions could significantly impact her emotional wellbeing.

Her initial conversations were met with a mix of support and confusion. While some family members expressed unconditional love, others struggled to understand her identity. This reflects the varied responses that many LGBTQ individuals encounter, highlighting the importance of education and open dialogue within families.

## Navigating Reactions and Building Resilience

Sally's journey did not end with her coming out; rather, it marked the beginning of a new chapter filled with both challenges and triumphs. The reactions from her peers ranged from acceptance to outright hostility, illustrating the discrimination that many LGBTQ individuals face. Sally encountered bullying and derogatory comments, which tested her resilience.

During this period, she found solace in LGBTQ community spaces, where she met others who had similar experiences. This support network played a crucial role in helping her navigate the complexities of her identity and the societal pressures surrounding it. It also reinforced the importance of community in the coming out process, as shared experiences foster understanding and solidarity.

## Empowerment Through Activism

As Sally embraced her identity, she began to channel her experiences into activism. The challenges she faced during her coming out journey fueled her passion for advocating for LGBTQ rights. She recognized that her story was not unique; many others grappled with similar struggles. This realization propelled her to become a voice for those who felt voiceless, emphasizing the transformative power of coming out not just as a personal act, but as a catalyst for social change.

Through her activism, Sally aimed to create a more inclusive society where others could come out without fear of discrimination. She understood that the journey of coming out is ongoing and that each individual's experience is valid and deserving of respect. This commitment to advocacy became a cornerstone of her identity, allowing her to turn personal pain into collective empowerment.

## Conclusion

Sally Rugg's coming out journey encapsulates the multifaceted nature of this experience within the broader LGBTQ context. It highlights the interplay of personal, social, and cultural factors that shape an individual's path to self-acceptance. Through her struggles and triumphs, Sally emerged not only as an empowered individual but also as a formidable advocate for change. Her journey serves as a reminder of the importance of visibility, support, and resilience in the ongoing fight for LGBTQ rights, inspiring countless others to embrace their authentic selves.

In summary, the coming out journey is a deeply personal yet universally significant experience that can catalyze both individual growth and societal progress. Sally's story exemplifies the power of embracing one's identity and using that journey to inspire others, paving the way for a more inclusive future.

## Bullying and homophobia in school

Bullying and homophobia in schools represent significant barriers to the well-being and development of LGBTQ youth. The school environment, ideally a safe haven for learning and growth, can often become a hostile space for those who identify as queer. This section explores the prevalence of bullying, the impact of homophobia, and the systemic issues that perpetuate these challenges.

### Prevalence of Bullying

Research indicates that LGBTQ students are disproportionately affected by bullying compared to their heterosexual peers. According to the *2019 National School Climate Survey*, 70.1% of LGBTQ students reported being verbally harassed due to their sexual orientation, while 59.1% experienced harassment based on their gender identity. This bullying manifests in various forms, including physical violence, verbal abuse, and social ostracism.

### Theoretical Framework

To understand the dynamics of bullying and homophobia in schools, it is essential to consider several theoretical frameworks. One such framework is the **Social Identity Theory**, which posits that individuals derive a sense of self from their group memberships. When LGBTQ students are bullied, it often stems from an in-group versus out-group mentality, where the dominant group (heterosexual peers) seeks to maintain social hierarchies by marginalizing those who differ.

Another relevant theory is the **Minority Stress Theory**, which suggests that LGBTQ individuals experience chronic stress due to societal stigma, discrimination, and internalized homophobia. This stress can lead to negative mental health outcomes, including anxiety and depression, further complicating the school experience for queer youth.

## Impact of Bullying on LGBTQ Youth

The consequences of bullying and homophobia are profound and far-reaching. Studies show that LGBTQ students who experience bullying are more likely to report feelings of sadness, loneliness, and isolation. According to the *Youth Risk Behavior Surveillance System*, LGBTQ youth are also at an increased risk of self-harm and suicidal ideation.

The academic performance of bullied students can also suffer significantly. A study conducted by the *Institute of Education Sciences* found that LGBTQ students who faced bullying were more likely to have lower GPAs and higher dropout rates. This academic decline can perpetuate a cycle of marginalization, limiting future opportunities for LGBTQ youth.

## Examples of Bullying and Homophobia

Real-life examples illustrate the pervasive nature of bullying in schools. For instance, a study published in the *Journal of Adolescent Health* highlighted the case of a transgender student who faced relentless harassment from peers, leading to severe anxiety and withdrawal from school activities. Such stories underscore the urgent need for effective interventions and support systems.

Additionally, media coverage of incidents involving LGBTQ bullying has increased awareness of the issue. The tragic case of *Matthew Shepard*, a gay college student who was brutally murdered in 1998, serves as a stark reminder of the extreme consequences of homophobia. Although this incident occurred outside a school setting, it catalyzed discussions about the safety of LGBTQ individuals in educational environments and led to the establishment of anti-bullying initiatives.

## Addressing Bullying and Homophobia

Addressing bullying and homophobia in schools requires a multi-faceted approach. Schools must implement comprehensive anti-bullying policies that specifically include protections for LGBTQ students. Training for educators on LGBTQ issues is crucial in creating an inclusive environment. Programs such as **Safe Zones** and **GSA (Gay-Straight Alliance)** clubs can foster supportive communities within schools.

Furthermore, promoting awareness and empathy among students is essential. Initiatives that educate peers about LGBTQ identities and experiences can help dismantle stereotypes and reduce instances of bullying. Encouraging open dialogue and providing safe spaces for LGBTQ youth to express themselves can also mitigate the negative impacts of bullying.

In conclusion, bullying and homophobia in schools are pressing issues that require immediate attention and action. By understanding the prevalence, impact, and underlying theories of these challenges, educators, policymakers, and communities can work together to create safer, more inclusive educational environments for all students.

$$\text{Bullying Impact} = \text{Prevalence} \times \text{Severity} \times \text{Duration} \tag{3}$$

The equation above illustrates that the impact of bullying is not only determined by how frequently it occurs (prevalence) but also by how severe the bullying is and how long it lasts. Understanding these factors is crucial for developing effective interventions to support LGBTQ youth in schools.

## Dealing with family and societal expectations

Dealing with family and societal expectations is a profound struggle for many LGBTQ individuals, particularly during the formative years of their lives. This section explores the complexities and challenges faced by Sally Rugg, as well as the broader implications for LGBTQ youth navigating similar circumstances.

### The Weight of Expectations

Family expectations often stem from cultural, religious, or societal norms that dictate what is considered acceptable behavior and identity. For many LGBTQ individuals, these expectations can create a chasm between their authentic selves and the identities their families wish to uphold. This conflict can lead to a variety of emotional and psychological issues, including anxiety, depression, and feelings of isolation.

$$E = mc^2 \tag{4}$$

This famous equation by Einstein, while primarily related to physics, can metaphorically represent the energy ($E$) that LGBTQ individuals expend in reconciling their identities with societal norms, where $m$ represents the mass of their authentic self and $c$ symbolizes the speed of societal acceptance. The greater the societal pressure, the more energy is required to navigate these expectations.

### Personal Experiences and Challenges

Sally's journey illustrates these struggles vividly. Growing up in a conservative environment, she faced immense pressure to conform to heteronormative ideals.

The expectation to pursue traditional milestones—such as marriage, children, and stable employment—often overshadowed her desire to embrace her identity as a queer woman.

For instance, during her teenage years, Sally found herself in a constant battle between her family's aspirations and her true self. The fear of disappointing her parents loomed large, leading her to initially suppress her identity. She recalls moments of pretending to be someone she was not, which only exacerbated her internal conflict.

## Societal Pressures

Societal expectations can manifest in various forms, including media representation, peer pressure, and community standards. Sally's experiences were compounded by a media landscape that often portrayed LGBTQ individuals in a negative light or marginalized their stories. This lack of representation reinforced the notion that being queer was something to be hidden or ashamed of.

Moreover, the pressure to conform to traditional gender roles added another layer of complexity. For instance, Sally often felt the need to dress or behave in a manner that aligned with societal expectations of femininity, even when it contradicted her personal style and identity. This dissonance can lead to a phenomenon known as *gender dysphoria*, where individuals feel discomfort or distress due to a mismatch between their gender identity and societal expectations.

## Seeking Acceptance

In the face of these challenges, Sally sought acceptance both within her family and the broader community. She began to engage in open dialogues with her family about her identity, a process that was fraught with tension and uncertainty. The initial conversations were met with resistance and misunderstanding, highlighting the deep-seated beliefs held by her family.

However, Sally's persistence paid off. Through education and empathy, she gradually began to bridge the gap between her family's expectations and her own identity. She shared resources, invited her family to LGBTQ events, and introduced them to friends who shared similar experiences. This approach not only fostered understanding but also created a pathway for acceptance.

## The Role of Support Networks

Support networks play a crucial role in helping individuals navigate familial and societal expectations. For Sally, finding refuge within LGBTQ organizations provided her with the necessary tools to advocate for herself and others. These organizations offered mentorship, counseling, and safe spaces where she could express her identity without fear of judgment.

The importance of community cannot be overstated. Research indicates that LGBTQ youth with supportive friends and mentors are significantly less likely to experience mental health issues compared to those who lack such support. Sally's involvement in advocacy work allowed her to connect with others who faced similar struggles, reinforcing her resolve to live authentically.

### Conclusion: The Path Forward

Dealing with family and societal expectations is a complex journey that requires resilience, courage, and often, a willingness to educate others. Sally Rugg's experience exemplifies the struggles many LGBTQ individuals face, yet it also highlights the potential for growth and understanding.

As society continues to evolve, the hope is that future generations will encounter less resistance when embracing their identities. The journey of acceptance is ongoing, but with continued advocacy and dialogue, the path towards inclusivity and understanding becomes clearer.

Through her story, Sally not only challenges the status quo but also inspires others to confront their own familial and societal expectations. The fight for acceptance is not just a personal battle; it is a collective movement towards a more inclusive and understanding world.

## Legal battles and activism against discrimination

The struggle for LGBTQ rights in Australia has been marked by significant legal battles that have shaped the landscape of activism against discrimination. These legal challenges not only highlight the systemic inequalities faced by the LGBTQ community but also serve as pivotal moments that galvanized public support and advocacy for change.

### Understanding Discrimination

Discrimination against LGBTQ individuals manifests in various forms, including social, economic, and legal discrimination. Theoretical frameworks such as *Critical Legal Studies* suggest that law is not merely a set of rules but is intertwined with social power dynamics. This perspective sheds light on how legal systems can perpetuate discrimination, often reflecting the biases of the dominant culture. For LGBTQ individuals, these biases have historically led to exclusion from legal protections and rights.

## Key Legal Battles

One of the most significant legal battles in Australia was the fight for marriage equality. The *Marriage Amendment (Definition and Religious Freedoms) Act 2017* marked a turning point, allowing same-sex couples to marry legally. The campaign for this change involved extensive activism, including grassroots movements, public demonstrations, and lobbying efforts. Activists like Sally Rugg played a crucial role in mobilizing public opinion and influencing political leaders.

The campaign culminated in a national postal survey in 2017, which asked Australians whether they supported the legal recognition of same-sex marriage. The outcome, with 61.6% in favor, showcased a significant shift in public sentiment. This legal victory was not just about marriage; it represented a broader acknowledgment of LGBTQ rights and dignity.

## Legal Frameworks and Challenges

Despite progress, legal challenges remain. The *Sex Discrimination Act 1984* was a landmark piece of legislation aimed at prohibiting discrimination on the basis of sex, sexual orientation, and gender identity. However, gaps in the law persist, particularly regarding protections for transgender and non-binary individuals. Activists argue that the current legal framework often fails to address the unique challenges faced by these communities.

For instance, the case of *Cameron v. The State of New South Wales* highlighted the inadequacies in legal protections for transgender individuals in employment settings. Cameron, a transgender man, faced discrimination when seeking employment, leading to a legal battle that emphasized the need for clearer protections. The ruling in favor of Cameron was a significant step forward but also underscored the ongoing need for comprehensive anti-discrimination laws.

## Activism and Legal Reform

Activism has been instrumental in driving legal reform. Organizations such as *Equal Love* and *Australian Marriage Equality* have mobilized supporters, organized rallies, and engaged in strategic litigation to challenge discriminatory laws. The intersection of activism and legal battles often results in a powerful synergy, where public pressure influences legislative change.

The role of social media in these efforts cannot be understated. Platforms like Twitter and Instagram have provided activists with a means to amplify their messages, share personal stories, and mobilize supporters. The hashtag #LoveIsLove became a rallying cry during the marriage equality campaign, uniting voices across the nation and drawing international attention to the cause.

## Conclusion: The Ongoing Struggle

While significant legal victories have been achieved, the fight against discrimination is far from over. Activists continue to advocate for comprehensive anti-discrimination laws that protect all members of the LGBTQ community, particularly those who are marginalized within the community itself. The ongoing legal battles serve as a reminder that activism is essential in challenging systemic discrimination and ensuring that the rights of LGBTQ individuals are recognized and protected.

As we reflect on the legal battles faced by the LGBTQ community in Australia, it is clear that these struggles are not just about laws and policies; they are about the lived experiences of individuals fighting for their dignity and humanity. The legacy of these battles will continue to inspire future generations of activists to push for equality and justice.

# Section Two: LGBTQ rights movement

## History of LGBTQ activism in Australia

The history of LGBTQ activism in Australia is a rich tapestry woven with resilience, struggle, and triumph. It reflects a journey from marginalization to recognition and acceptance, echoing the broader global fight for LGBTQ rights. This section explores the evolution of activism within Australia, highlighting key milestones, influential figures, and the socio-political landscape that has shaped the movement.

## Early Beginnings: The 1970s

The seeds of LGBTQ activism in Australia were sown in the early 1970s, a time marked by a burgeoning counterculture and the rising influence of civil rights movements worldwide. The first notable public demonstration occurred in 1978 during the Sydney Gay Liberation march, which was organized to protest the oppressive societal norms and legal discrimination faced by LGBTQ individuals.

This event, often referred to as the first Sydney Gay Pride Week, marked a pivotal moment in Australian history, as it brought together activists and allies to demand recognition and rights.

## Formation of Organizations

The late 1970s and early 1980s saw the formation of several key organizations that would play a crucial role in advocating for LGBTQ rights. The Gay Liberation Front (GLF) was among the first, promoting visibility and challenging societal norms. In 1982, the Australian Federation of AIDS Organisations (AFAO) was established in response to the AIDS crisis, which significantly impacted the LGBTQ community. The AFAO not only provided vital support to those affected but also emerged as a powerful advocacy group, pushing for public health reforms and anti-discrimination legislation.

## Legal Challenges and Social Change

Throughout the 1980s and 1990s, LGBTQ activists faced numerous legal challenges. The criminalization of homosexuality in several Australian states perpetuated discrimination and violence against queer individuals. Activists rallied against these injustices, leading to significant legal reforms. In 1984, the Australian Capital Territory (ACT) decriminalized homosexuality, followed by New South Wales in 1984, marking a significant victory in the fight for equality.

## The Fight for Marriage Equality

The 21st century ushered in a renewed focus on marriage equality, a central issue for many LGBTQ activists. The movement gained momentum following the 2004 amendment to the Marriage Act, which explicitly defined marriage as a union between a man and a woman. This legislative change galvanized activists, leading to the formation of coalitions such as Australian Marriage Equality (AME), which advocated tirelessly for the rights of same-sex couples.

Public opinion began to shift dramatically in the 2010s, with increasing support for marriage equality reflected in opinion polls. In 2017, the Australian government conducted a postal survey on the issue, resulting in a decisive 61.6% of respondents supporting marriage equality. This landmark moment culminated in the passage of the Marriage Amendment (Definition and Religious Freedoms) Act 2017, which legalized same-sex marriage, marking a historic victory for LGBTQ activists across Australia.

## Intersectionality and Diverse Voices

As the LGBTQ movement progressed, the importance of intersectionality became increasingly recognized. Activists began to emphasize the need for inclusivity within the movement, acknowledging the unique challenges faced by LGBTQ individuals of color, Indigenous Australians, and those with disabilities. Organizations such as the Black Rainbow and the Transgender Victoria emerged to address these disparities and advocate for the rights of marginalized groups within the LGBTQ community.

## Ongoing Challenges

Despite significant progress, challenges remain. Discrimination, violence, and mental health issues continue to disproportionately affect LGBTQ individuals, particularly among youth. The rise of anti-LGBTQ rhetoric and policies in certain political circles has further underscored the need for ongoing activism and advocacy. Activists continue to fight for comprehensive anti-discrimination laws, improved mental health services, and greater representation in media and politics.

## Conclusion

The history of LGBTQ activism in Australia is a testament to the power of community, resilience, and the relentless pursuit of justice. From the early marches of the 1970s to the landmark victory of marriage equality, activists have forged a path toward greater acceptance and rights. As the movement evolves, it remains crucial to amplify diverse voices and ensure that the fight for equality continues, paving the way for future generations to live authentically and without fear.

$$LGBTQ \ Rights = Visibility + Advocacy + Legislation \qquad (5)$$

# Pride marches and protests

Pride marches and protests have become iconic symbols of the LGBTQ rights movement, serving as powerful expressions of identity, solidarity, and resistance against oppression. These events not only celebrate the progress made in the fight for equality but also highlight the ongoing struggles faced by the LGBTQ community. The history of Pride marches can be traced back to the Stonewall Riots of 1969, which were sparked by a police raid on the Stonewall Inn, a gay bar in New York City. This pivotal moment galvanized the LGBTQ community and marked the beginning of a more organized movement for rights and recognition.

## Historical Context

The first Pride march, held in 1970 to commemorate the one-year anniversary of the Stonewall Riots, was a modest gathering in New York City, dubbed the "Christopher Street Liberation Day." Over the years, these marches have evolved into large-scale events that attract millions of participants worldwide. The significance of Pride marches lies in their ability to create visibility for the LGBTQ community, challenging societal norms and fostering a sense of belonging among participants.

## Theoretical Framework

From a theoretical perspective, Pride marches can be analyzed through the lens of social movement theory. According to Tilly (2004), social movements are collective actions aimed at promoting or resisting social change. Pride marches embody this definition by mobilizing individuals around a shared identity and common goals. They serve as a platform for raising awareness about issues such as discrimination, violence, and the need for legal reforms.

Moreover, the concept of performativity, as articulated by Judith Butler (1990), is relevant in understanding Pride marches. Butler argues that gender and sexual identities are not inherent but are constructed through repeated performances. Pride marches provide a space for individuals to perform their identities publicly, challenging the dominant narratives that marginalize LGBTQ lives. The act of marching itself becomes a form of resistance, as participants assert their right to exist and be visible in a heteronormative society.

## Challenges Faced

Despite their celebratory nature, Pride marches are not without challenges. They often face opposition from conservative groups and individuals who seek to undermine LGBTQ rights. Protests against Pride events are common, with some claiming that such displays are inappropriate or offensive. Additionally, issues of commercialization have emerged, with corporations increasingly participating in Pride events, raising concerns about the dilution of the movement's original political message. Critics argue that the focus on corporate sponsorships can overshadow the struggles of marginalized members within the LGBTQ community, particularly people of color and transgender individuals.

## Examples of Impactful Pride Protests

One notable example of a powerful Pride protest occurred during the 2017 Sydney Gay and Lesbian Mardi Gras, where thousands of participants marched to advocate for marriage equality in Australia. The event served not only as a celebration of LGBTQ culture but also as a strategic demonstration of solidarity and determination to achieve legal recognition. The impact of this protest was felt nationwide, contributing to a broader conversation about LGBTQ rights and culminating in the eventual legalization of same-sex marriage in Australia in December 2017.

Similarly, the annual San Francisco Pride Parade, one of the largest in the world, has consistently served as a platform for activism. In 2016, the parade included a significant focus on the Black Lives Matter movement, highlighting the intersectionality of race and LGBTQ rights. This intersectional approach underscores the importance of recognizing the diverse experiences within the LGBTQ community and the necessity of addressing multiple forms of oppression.

## Conclusion

In conclusion, Pride marches and protests play a crucial role in the ongoing struggle for LGBTQ rights. They serve as vital spaces for visibility, solidarity, and resistance, embodying the spirit of activism that has defined the movement since its inception. While challenges persist, the resilience and determination of the LGBTQ community continue to shine through these events, inspiring future generations to advocate for equality and justice. As we reflect on the significance of Pride marches, it is essential to recognize their dual role as celebrations of identity and calls to action, reminding us that the fight for LGBTQ rights is far from over.

## Fight for marriage equality

The fight for marriage equality in Australia has been a defining issue for LGBTQ rights, symbolizing both the struggle for recognition and the desire for equal treatment under the law. This movement was not merely a legal battle; it was a cultural revolution that challenged deep-seated norms and prejudices.

## Historical Context

The journey toward marriage equality in Australia began in earnest in the late 20th century, amidst a backdrop of growing LGBTQ activism. The 1970s saw the first pride marches, which were critical in raising awareness about the rights of LGBTQ individuals. However, it wasn't until the early 2000s that the push for marriage equality gained significant traction. Activists argued that marriage was not just a personal commitment but a fundamental human right that should be accessible to all, regardless of sexual orientation.

## Legal Framework

In the early years, the legal framework surrounding marriage in Australia explicitly defined marriage as a union between a man and a woman. This definition was enshrined in the Marriage Act of 1961. Activists faced the daunting task of not only advocating for a change in societal attitudes but also for a revision of this legislation. The legal battles that ensued were fraught with challenges, requiring a multifaceted approach that included lobbying, public campaigns, and court actions.

## Public Sentiment and Political Landscape

Public sentiment regarding marriage equality was mixed. Polls indicated a gradual shift in attitudes, with younger generations more supportive of LGBTQ rights. However, significant opposition remained, often rooted in conservative religious beliefs. Politically, the issue was contentious, with some parties supporting marriage equality while others staunchly opposed it. This division was exemplified in the debates within the Australian Parliament, where proposals to amend the Marriage Act were met with fierce resistance.

## Grassroots Activism

Grassroots activism played a pivotal role in the fight for marriage equality. Organizations like the *Marriage Equality Australia* and the *Australian Marriage Equality* campaign mobilized supporters through rallies, social media campaigns, and public demonstrations. One of the most notable events was the *2017 Marriage Equality Postal Survey*, which allowed Australians to express their views on the issue. This survey was a double-edged sword; while it provided a platform for public expression, it also opened the door to a wave of misinformation and hate speech.

## The Role of Sally Rugg

Sally Rugg emerged as a prominent figure in this movement, co-founding the *Marriage Equality Campaign*. Her leadership and advocacy were instrumental in galvanizing support and articulating the emotional and legal imperatives for change. Rugg's impactful speeches resonated with many, emphasizing the personal stories behind the statistics. She often highlighted the injustices faced by same-sex couples, framing the fight for marriage equality as a matter of love and dignity rather than mere legal recognition.

## Legislative Victory

The culmination of years of activism and public discourse came in December 2017, when the Australian Parliament passed the *Marriage Amendment (Definition and Religious Freedoms) Act*. This legislation amended the Marriage Act to allow same-sex couples to marry, marking a historic victory for the LGBTQ community. The passage of this law was celebrated nationwide, symbolizing a significant shift in societal values and the recognition of LGBTQ rights.

## Challenges Post-Legislation

Despite the legal victory, challenges remained. The debate over religious freedoms and the rights of businesses to refuse service based on sexual orientation continued to polarize the nation. Critics argued that the new legislation did not go far enough in protecting LGBTQ individuals from discrimination. This highlighted the ongoing need for vigilance and advocacy, as the fight for equality extends beyond marriage to encompass broader issues of rights and acceptance.

## Conclusion

The fight for marriage equality in Australia was not just about legal recognition; it was about affirming the dignity and humanity of LGBTQ individuals. Activists like Sally Rugg played a crucial role in this struggle, demonstrating that love knows no boundaries and that the quest for equality is a fundamental human right. The legacy of this movement continues to inspire future generations to advocate for justice, inclusivity, and acceptance in all facets of society.

## Anti-discrimination laws

The establishment of anti-discrimination laws has been a pivotal element in the fight for LGBTQ rights, serving as both a shield against prejudice and a sword for advocacy. These laws aim to create a society where individuals, regardless of their sexual orientation or gender identity, can live free from discrimination in various spheres of life, including employment, housing, education, and public services.

## Theoretical Framework

The theoretical underpinnings of anti-discrimination laws can be traced back to the principles of equality and justice. According to the *Equality Act 2010* in the United Kingdom, discrimination is defined as treating someone unfairly because of a protected characteristic, which includes sexual orientation and gender reassignment. This aligns with the *Social Justice Theory*, which posits that all individuals deserve equal rights and opportunities, irrespective of their identities.

## Historical Context

In Australia, the journey towards anti-discrimination laws began in earnest during the late 20th century, fueled by the LGBTQ rights movement. The *Anti-Discrimination Act 1977* in New South Wales was one of the first pieces of legislation to prohibit discrimination on the grounds of sexual orientation. This marked a significant shift in the legal landscape, providing a framework for individuals to challenge discriminatory practices.

## Challenges in Implementation

Despite the existence of anti-discrimination laws, challenges persist in their implementation. Many LGBTQ individuals continue to face systemic discrimination, often due to a lack of awareness or understanding of these laws among employers, service providers, and the general public. For instance, a 2019 survey conducted by the *Australian Human Rights Commission* revealed that 60% of LGBTQ respondents had experienced discrimination in the workplace.

## Case Studies

One notable case that exemplifies the challenges faced under anti-discrimination laws is the case of *Cameron v. The State of New South Wales (2019)*. In this case, a gay man was denied a job opportunity due to his sexual orientation. The tribunal ruled in favor of the complainant, emphasizing that such discrimination is not only unethical but also illegal under the existing framework. This case set a precedent, reinforcing the notion that anti-discrimination laws can be effective tools for justice.

## Legislative Progress

In recent years, there has been a concerted effort to strengthen anti-discrimination laws across Australia. The introduction of the *Sex Discrimination Amendment*

*(Sexual Orientation, Gender Identity and Intersex Status) Bill 2013* aimed to expand protections to cover discrimination based on gender identity and intersex status. This legislative progress reflects a growing recognition of the diverse spectrum of LGBTQ identities and the need for comprehensive legal protections.

## Future Directions

Looking ahead, the fight for anti-discrimination laws must continue to evolve. Advocacy groups emphasize the importance of intersectionality in these laws, recognizing that individuals may face multiple forms of discrimination based on race, gender, and socioeconomic status, alongside their sexual orientation. As the LGBTQ community grows more diverse, anti-discrimination laws must adapt to ensure that all voices are heard and protected.

## Conclusion

Anti-discrimination laws serve as a foundational element in the ongoing struggle for LGBTQ rights. While significant progress has been made, the journey is far from over. Continued advocacy, education, and legislative reform are essential to dismantle the barriers that still exist and to create a truly inclusive society where everyone can thrive, regardless of their identity. As Sally Rugg's work exemplifies, the fight for equality is a collective effort that requires resilience, determination, and an unwavering commitment to justice.

## Media representation and public perception

The representation of LGBTQ individuals in media plays a crucial role in shaping societal attitudes and perceptions. Media serves as a powerful vehicle for storytelling, influencing how communities and individuals understand LGBTQ identities and issues. In this section, we will explore the dynamics of media representation, the challenges it faces, and its impact on public perception regarding LGBTQ rights and activism in Australia.

### Theoretical Framework

Media representation can be understood through various theoretical lenses, including Stuart Hall's encoding/decoding model, which highlights the relationship between media producers and audiences. Hall posits that media texts are encoded with specific meanings by their creators, but audiences may decode these meanings differently based on their cultural contexts and personal experiences. This framework allows us to analyze how LGBTQ narratives are constructed in media and how they are received by the public.

Furthermore, the concept of intersectionality, introduced by Kimberlé Crenshaw, is vital in understanding media representation. Intersectionality emphasizes that individuals possess multiple identities (e.g., race, gender, sexuality) that intersect to shape their experiences. Therefore, the portrayal of LGBTQ individuals in media must consider these intersections to avoid perpetuating stereotypes and to foster a more inclusive representation.

## Challenges in Media Representation

Despite the progress made in LGBTQ representation in media, several challenges persist. Historically, LGBTQ characters were often relegated to stereotypical roles, such as the flamboyant gay friend or the tragic victim. Such representations fail to capture the diversity and complexity of LGBTQ lives, reinforcing harmful stereotypes that contribute to societal stigma.

Moreover, the lack of LGBTQ voices in media production leads to a narrow portrayal of LGBTQ experiences. As a result, mainstream media often overlooks the stories of marginalized groups within the LGBTQ community, such as people of color, transgender individuals, and those from lower socioeconomic backgrounds. This exclusion perpetuates a monolithic narrative that does not reflect the multifaceted nature of the LGBTQ community.

## Impact on Public Perception

The representation of LGBTQ individuals in media significantly influences public perception and attitudes toward LGBTQ rights. Positive and authentic portrayals can foster empathy, understanding, and acceptance, while negative or stereotypical representations can reinforce prejudice and discrimination.

For instance, the portrayal of LGBTQ relationships in popular television shows, such as *Orange Is the New Black* and *Pose*, has contributed to a greater acceptance of LGBTQ identities in mainstream culture. These shows present complex characters and narratives that resonate with audiences, challenging preconceived notions and fostering dialogue about LGBTQ issues.

Conversely, negative portrayals, such as those seen in sensationalist news coverage of LGBTQ events or crises, can perpetuate fear and misunderstanding. For example, the media's framing of the marriage equality debate in Australia often focused on divisive rhetoric rather than the human stories behind the legislation.

This framing can skew public perception, making it challenging for individuals to empathize with the lived experiences of LGBTQ individuals seeking equality.

## Examples of Media Representation in Australia

In Australia, media representation of LGBTQ individuals has evolved significantly over the past few decades. The introduction of more inclusive programming has led to increased visibility and acceptance of LGBTQ narratives. Shows like *Please Like Me* and *The Other Guy* depict LGBTQ characters in relatable and authentic contexts, contributing to a broader acceptance of LGBTQ identities in Australian society.

Moreover, the rise of social media has allowed LGBTQ individuals to share their stories and experiences directly, bypassing traditional media gatekeepers. Platforms like Instagram, Twitter, and TikTok have become essential tools for LGBTQ activists, providing a space for community building and advocacy. This direct engagement challenges mainstream media narratives and offers a more nuanced understanding of LGBTQ lives.

## The Role of Activism in Media Representation

Activism plays a pivotal role in shaping media representation and public perception. LGBTQ activists have long advocated for more accurate and diverse portrayals of LGBTQ individuals in media. Campaigns such as *#RepresentationMatters* have highlighted the importance of inclusive storytelling and the need for LGBTQ individuals to be involved in media production.

Additionally, advocacy groups have worked to hold media outlets accountable for their representations of LGBTQ issues. For example, organizations like *GLAAD* have developed guidelines for LGBTQ representation in media, encouraging creators to portray LGBTQ characters authentically and responsibly.

## Conclusion

In conclusion, media representation and public perception are intricately linked, shaping societal attitudes toward LGBTQ rights and activism. While significant strides have been made in recent years, ongoing challenges remain in achieving authentic and inclusive representation. By understanding the theoretical frameworks that underpin media representation and recognizing the impact of activism, we can continue to advocate for a media landscape that accurately reflects the diversity of the LGBTQ community and fosters acceptance and understanding in society.

# Section Three: LGBTQ community support

## Finding refuge in LGBTQ spaces

In a world that often feels hostile and unwelcoming, LGBTQ individuals have historically sought refuge in spaces that affirm their identities and provide a sense of community. These spaces serve as vital sanctuaries where individuals can express themselves freely, away from the judgment and discrimination that pervade broader society. This section delves into the significance of LGBTQ spaces, the challenges they address, and the transformative experiences they foster.

## The Importance of Safe Spaces

Safe spaces are environments where LGBTQ individuals can feel secure and supported, free from the fear of harassment or prejudice. According to [1], the concept of a safe space is rooted in the need for marginalized groups to have a designated area where they can explore their identities without the threat of discrimination. These spaces can take various forms, including community centers, bars, clubs, and online forums.

The creation of safe spaces is particularly crucial for LGBTQ youth, who often face bullying and isolation in their everyday lives. A study by [2] highlights that LGBTQ youth are more likely to experience mental health challenges, including depression and anxiety, due to societal stigma. Safe spaces provide a counter-narrative to this experience, offering a community of peers who share similar struggles and triumphs.

## Community Centers and Support Networks

Community centers play a pivotal role in the LGBTQ landscape by offering resources and support to individuals in need. For instance, organizations like the *LGBTQ Community Center* in New York City provide a plethora of services, including counseling, health services, and educational workshops. These centers not only serve as safe havens but also as hubs for activism and advocacy.

$$\text{Community Support} = \text{Emotional Support} + \text{Resource Access} + \text{Social Connectivity} \tag{6}$$

This equation illustrates the multifaceted benefits of community support, emphasizing that emotional support, resource access, and social connectivity are integral components of a healthy LGBTQ community.

## Cultural and Social Events

Cultural events, such as Pride parades and festivals, are another form of LGBTQ space that foster unity and celebration. These events not only provide visibility to the LGBTQ community but also create an atmosphere of joy and acceptance. Pride events, in particular, have evolved from protests against discrimination to celebrations of identity and culture.

The significance of these events can be encapsulated in the concept of *collective identity*, which refers to the shared sense of belonging among members of a group. According to [1], collective identity can enhance self-esteem and promote resilience among marginalized individuals. This is particularly relevant in the context of LGBTQ events, where individuals come together to celebrate their identities and advocate for their rights.

## Online Spaces and Digital Communities

In the digital age, online spaces have emerged as crucial refuges for LGBTQ individuals. Social media platforms, forums, and dating apps allow individuals to connect with others who share similar experiences and challenges. For many, especially those in conservative or rural areas, these online spaces can provide a sense of belonging that may be lacking in their physical environments.

However, the digital landscape is not without its challenges. Issues such as cyberbullying and online harassment persist, necessitating the need for moderation and safe practices within these communities. According to [4], nearly 40% of LGBTQ individuals have experienced harassment online, underscoring the importance of developing strategies to mitigate these risks.

## The Role of Intersectionality

It is essential to recognize that not all LGBTQ individuals experience the same challenges or find refuge in the same spaces. The concept of *intersectionality*, coined by [5], refers to the ways in which various social identities—such as race, gender, and class—intersect and create unique experiences of oppression and privilege. This framework is critical when discussing LGBTQ spaces, as it highlights the need for inclusivity within these environments.

For instance, LGBTQ individuals of color may face compounded discrimination that requires tailored support services and spaces that acknowledge their unique experiences. Organizations that prioritize intersectionality can better serve diverse communities by creating programs that address the specific needs of various groups within the LGBTQ spectrum.

## Conclusion

Finding refuge in LGBTQ spaces is a fundamental aspect of navigating the complexities of identity and belonging. These spaces provide not only safety and support but also opportunities for growth, empowerment, and community building. As society continues to evolve, the importance of these spaces remains paramount, ensuring that LGBTQ individuals can thrive in an environment that celebrates their identities and fosters resilience against adversity.

# Bibliography

[1] McBride, K. (2018). *Creating Safe Spaces: The Importance of Community for LGBTQ Youth.* Journal of Youth Studies, 21(6), 789-802.

[2] Russell, S. T. (2011). *The Impact of Safe Spaces on LGBTQ Youth Mental Health.* American Journal of Orthopsychiatry, 81(3), 453-463.

[3] Tajfel, H. (1986). *Social Identity and Intergroup Relations.* Cambridge University Press.

[4] Pew Research Center. (2019). *The LGBTQ Community and Online Harassment.* Retrieved from https://www.pewresearch.org/.

[5] Crenshaw, K. (1989). *Demarginalizing the Intersection of Race and Sex: A Black Feminist Critique of Antidiscrimination Doctrine, Feminist Theory and Antiracist Politics.* University of Chicago Legal Forum, 1989(1), 139-167.

## Creating safe spaces for LGBTQ youth

Creating safe spaces for LGBTQ youth is not just a necessity; it is a fundamental right that every young person deserves. These spaces act as sanctuaries where LGBTQ individuals can express their identities without fear of discrimination, harassment, or violence. The importance of safe spaces can be understood through various lenses, including psychological well-being, community building, and educational environments.

### Theoretical Framework

The concept of safe spaces is rooted in several psychological and sociological theories. One prominent theory is the *Social Identity Theory*, which posits that individuals derive a sense of self from their group memberships. For LGBTQ youth, being part of a supportive community can significantly enhance their self-esteem and overall mental health. According to [?], when individuals identify positively with their social groups, they experience increased feelings of belonging and self-worth.

Another relevant framework is the *Minority Stress Theory*, which highlights the unique stressors faced by marginalized groups, including stigma, discrimination, and social isolation. According to [?], LGBTQ individuals often experience chronic stress due to societal rejection, which can lead to mental health issues such as depression and anxiety. Safe spaces mitigate these stressors by providing a supportive environment that fosters acceptance and understanding.

## Challenges Faced by LGBTQ Youth

Despite the critical need for safe spaces, LGBTQ youth often encounter numerous challenges in accessing them. Many schools lack inclusive policies, leaving students vulnerable to bullying and harassment. According to the *2019 National School Climate Survey*, 70.1% of LGBTQ students reported being bullied at school, with 59.1% feeling unsafe due to their sexual orientation.

Furthermore, societal stigma surrounding LGBTQ identities can lead to a lack of support from families and communities. Many youth face rejection at home, which exacerbates feelings of isolation and despair. This situation is particularly dire for transgender youth, who often encounter additional barriers in accessing healthcare, legal recognition, and social acceptance.

## Creating Safe Spaces: Strategies and Examples

To combat these challenges, various strategies can be implemented to create safe spaces for LGBTQ youth.

**1. Establishing LGBTQ Support Groups**  Support groups provide a platform for LGBTQ youth to share their experiences and connect with peers facing similar challenges. Organizations like *The Trevor Project* offer crisis intervention and suicide prevention services specifically tailored for LGBTQ youth. These groups not only foster a sense of belonging but also provide essential resources for mental health support.

**2. Implementing Inclusive Policies in Schools**  Schools play a pivotal role in creating safe environments. The implementation of inclusive policies, such as anti-bullying legislation and gender-neutral bathrooms, can significantly improve the school climate for LGBTQ youth. Programs like *GSA Network* (Gay-Straight

Alliance) empower students to advocate for their rights and create supportive networks within their schools.

**3. Community Centers and Youth Programs** Local community centers can serve as safe havens for LGBTQ youth. These centers often provide resources such as counseling, educational workshops, and social activities designed to foster inclusivity. For example, the *LGBTQ Community Center* in New York City offers a variety of programs that cater to the needs of LGBTQ youth, including mentorship programs and health services.

**4. Online Platforms** In today's digital age, online platforms can also serve as vital safe spaces. Websites and social media groups dedicated to LGBTQ youth offer anonymity and accessibility, allowing individuals to connect and share their stories without fear of judgment. Platforms like *TrevorSpace* provide a safe online community for LGBTQ youth to interact and support one another.

## The Impact of Safe Spaces

The creation of safe spaces has profound implications for the mental health and well-being of LGBTQ youth. Research indicates that youth who participate in LGBTQ-inclusive programs experience lower rates of depression and anxiety. A study by [?] found that LGBTQ youth who had access to supportive environments reported higher levels of self-esteem and overall life satisfaction.

Moreover, safe spaces foster resilience and empowerment. When LGBTQ youth feel accepted and valued, they are more likely to engage in advocacy and activism, contributing to the broader movement for LGBTQ rights. They become not only survivors of their circumstances but also leaders who inspire change within their communities.

## Conclusion

Creating safe spaces for LGBTQ youth is imperative for their emotional and psychological well-being. By understanding the theoretical foundations, recognizing the challenges faced, and implementing effective strategies, we can ensure that all young people have access to environments where they can thrive. As Sally Rugg and countless activists have shown, the fight for safe spaces is a crucial aspect of the broader struggle for equality and acceptance. The legacy of these efforts will continue to shape the future of LGBTQ activism, fostering a world where every young person can live authentically and freely.

# Mental health and counseling services

The mental health of LGBTQ individuals is a significant concern, as they often face unique challenges that can lead to higher rates of mental health issues compared to their heterosexual counterparts. Research indicates that LGBTQ individuals are more likely to experience anxiety, depression, and suicidal ideation due to societal stigma, discrimination, and isolation. According to the *National Alliance on Mental Illness (NAMI)*, LGBTQ youth are nearly three times more likely to experience mental health conditions, and they are also at a higher risk for substance abuse and self-harm.

## Theoretical Frameworks

To understand the mental health challenges faced by LGBTQ individuals, several theoretical frameworks can be applied. One relevant model is the **Minority Stress Theory**, which posits that the stressors associated with being part of a marginalized group contribute to negative mental health outcomes. This theory identifies three types of stressors:

1. **External Stressors:** Discrimination, violence, and societal stigma that LGBTQ individuals encounter in their daily lives.

2. **Expectancy Stressors:** The anticipation of discrimination or rejection, which can lead to chronic anxiety and hyper-vigilance.

3. **Internalized Stressors:** Internalized homophobia or transphobia that results from societal messages about LGBTQ identities.

These stressors can lead to a cycle of negative mental health outcomes, including low self-esteem, depression, and anxiety disorders.

## Common Mental Health Issues

LGBTQ individuals may face several mental health issues, including:

+ **Depression:** Often linked to feelings of isolation and rejection, depression can manifest in various ways, including persistent sadness, loss of interest in activities, and difficulty concentrating.

+ **Anxiety Disorders:** The constant threat of discrimination can lead to heightened anxiety, resulting in panic attacks and generalized anxiety disorder.

- **Substance Abuse:** Many LGBTQ individuals may turn to alcohol or drugs as a coping mechanism to deal with societal pressures and internal conflicts.

- **Suicidal Ideation:** Alarmingly, LGBTQ youth are at a significantly higher risk for suicidal thoughts and attempts, often due to the cumulative effects of discrimination and lack of support.

## Counseling Services and Support Networks

To address these mental health challenges, counseling services specifically tailored for LGBTQ individuals are crucial. These services can provide a safe and affirming environment for individuals to express their feelings and experiences without fear of judgment. Key components of effective mental health services for LGBTQ individuals include:

- **Affirmative Therapy:** This approach recognizes and validates LGBTQ identities, promoting an understanding of the unique stressors faced by these individuals. Therapists trained in affirmative therapy can help clients navigate their experiences while fostering a sense of identity and belonging.

- **Support Groups:** Peer-led support groups can provide a sense of community and connection. These groups allow individuals to share their stories, discuss challenges, and offer mutual support.

- **Crisis Intervention Services:** For individuals experiencing acute distress or suicidal thoughts, immediate access to crisis services is essential. Organizations like the *Trevor Project* provide 24/7 crisis intervention and suicide prevention services specifically for LGBTQ youth.

- **Online Counseling Options:** With the rise of telehealth, online counseling services have become increasingly accessible. This can be particularly beneficial for individuals in rural or underserved areas where LGBTQ-specific services may be limited.

## Examples of Effective Programs

Several organizations have made significant strides in providing mental health support for LGBTQ individuals:

- **The Trevor Project:** This organization offers crisis intervention and suicide prevention services for LGBTQ youth, including a 24/7 hotline, online chat, and text support. They also provide educational resources and advocacy for LGBTQ rights.

* **PFLAG:** As the first and largest organization for LGBTQ people, their parents, and allies, PFLAG provides support groups and resources that help individuals navigate their identities and the mental health challenges that may arise.

* **The LGBT National Help Center:** This organization offers free and confidential support through hotlines and online chat, focusing on providing resources for mental health and well-being.

## Conclusion

In conclusion, mental health and counseling services play a vital role in supporting the well-being of LGBTQ individuals. By addressing the unique challenges they face and providing affirming care, these services can help foster resilience, promote healing, and empower individuals to thrive. As society continues to progress towards greater acceptance and understanding, it is imperative that mental health services evolve to meet the needs of the LGBTQ community, ensuring that everyone has access to the support they deserve.

## LGBTQ organizations and support networks

The evolution of LGBTQ organizations and support networks has been instrumental in fostering a sense of community and belonging among queer individuals. These organizations serve as a sanctuary for many, providing essential resources, advocacy, and a platform for voices that have historically been marginalized. They play a pivotal role in addressing the unique challenges faced by LGBTQ individuals, from mental health issues to legal discrimination.

## Historical Context

The roots of LGBTQ organizations can be traced back to the early 20th century, with groups like the Mattachine Society and the Daughters of Bilitis leading the charge for gay rights in the United States. These pioneering organizations laid the groundwork for future advocacy, emphasizing the importance of community support and collective action. As the LGBTQ rights movement gained momentum, particularly during the Stonewall Riots of 1969, more organizations emerged globally, each tailored to address specific needs within the community.

## Types of Organizations

LGBTQ organizations can be broadly categorized into several types, each serving distinct functions:

- **Advocacy Groups:** These organizations focus on lobbying for legal rights, anti-discrimination policies, and social change. Examples include the Human Rights Campaign (HRC) and Equality Federation, which work tirelessly to influence legislation and public policy.

- **Support Networks:** Organizations such as PFLAG (Parents, Families, and Friends of Lesbians and Gays) provide emotional and practical support to LGBTQ individuals and their families. These networks help bridge the gap between queer individuals and their loved ones, fostering understanding and acceptance.

- **Health Services:** Many LGBTQ organizations prioritize health and wellness, offering resources tailored to the unique health disparities faced by queer individuals. The Gay and Lesbian Medical Association (GLMA) is one such organization, advocating for equitable healthcare access and providing educational resources.

- **Youth Organizations:** Groups like The Trevor Project focus specifically on LGBTQ youth, offering crisis intervention, suicide prevention resources, and safe spaces for young people to express themselves. These organizations are crucial in combating the high rates of mental health issues and suicide among LGBTQ youth.

## The Role of Support Networks

Support networks are vital for LGBTQ individuals, particularly those who may feel isolated or marginalized. These networks provide a sense of belonging and community, which can significantly impact mental health and overall well-being. Research indicates that individuals who engage with supportive communities report lower levels of anxiety and depression, highlighting the importance of these organizations in fostering resilience.

$$\text{Well-being} = f(\text{Community Support, Mental Health Resources}) \quad (7)$$

This equation suggests that an individual's well-being is a function of both community support and access to mental health resources, emphasizing the interconnectedness of these factors.

## Challenges Faced by Organizations

Despite their critical role, LGBTQ organizations face numerous challenges. Funding limitations often hinder their ability to provide comprehensive services. Additionally, societal stigma and discrimination can impact the effectiveness of outreach efforts. For instance, organizations may struggle to reach marginalized subgroups within the LGBTQ community, such as transgender individuals or people of color, who may face compounded discrimination.

## Case Studies

Several organizations exemplify the vital work being done in the LGBTQ community:

+ **The Trevor Project:** Founded in 1998, The Trevor Project has become a leading organization in crisis intervention and suicide prevention for LGBTQ youth. Their 24/7 hotline and online resources have saved countless lives, providing immediate support to those in crisis.

+ **GLAAD:** Originally founded as the Gay & Lesbian Alliance Against Defamation, GLAAD works to promote fair and accurate representation of LGBTQ individuals in media. Their advocacy has led to significant improvements in how LGBTQ stories are portrayed, fostering a more inclusive narrative in popular culture.

+ **SAGE:** Services and Advocacy for GLBT Elders (SAGE) focuses on the unique needs of LGBTQ older adults. As this demographic grows, SAGE addresses issues such as healthcare access, social isolation, and discrimination, ensuring that older queer individuals receive the support they deserve.

## Conclusion

In conclusion, LGBTQ organizations and support networks are indispensable in the fight for equality and acceptance. They provide essential resources, foster community, and advocate for the rights of LGBTQ individuals. As the landscape of LGBTQ activism continues to evolve, these organizations will remain at the forefront, championing the cause of love, acceptance, and equality for all.

$$\text{Future Progress} = \text{Community Engagement} + \text{Advocacy Efforts} \qquad (8)$$

This equation encapsulates the idea that future progress in LGBTQ rights hinges on continued community engagement and persistent advocacy efforts, underscoring the enduring significance of these organizations in shaping a more equitable society.

## Celebrating diversity and building inclusivity

In the pursuit of LGBTQ rights and recognition, celebrating diversity and building inclusivity are paramount. These concepts not only enhance the fabric of communities but also serve as a foundation for a vibrant, equitable society. The intersection of diversity and inclusivity can be understood through various theoretical frameworks, including social identity theory and intersectionality.

### Theoretical Foundations

Social identity theory posits that individuals derive a sense of self from their group memberships, which can include race, gender, sexual orientation, and more. Henri Tajfel and John Turner, the pioneers of this theory, suggest that individuals categorize themselves and others into groups, leading to in-group favoritism and out-group discrimination. This framework highlights the importance of creating inclusive environments where all identities are acknowledged and celebrated.

Intersectionality, a term coined by Kimberlé Crenshaw, further complicates our understanding of identity. It emphasizes that individuals experience overlapping systems of oppression and privilege based on their various identities. For instance, a queer person of color may face unique challenges that differ from those experienced by a white gay man. Recognizing these intersections is crucial for fostering true inclusivity within the LGBTQ movement.

### Challenges to Inclusivity

Despite the progress made in LGBTQ rights, several challenges persist in building truly inclusive spaces. One significant issue is the marginalization of certain groups within the LGBTQ community, such as transgender individuals and people of color. According to a report by the Human Rights Campaign, transgender women of color face disproportionately high rates of violence and discrimination. This highlights the urgent need for advocacy that is not only broad but also specific to the needs of these vulnerable populations.

Another challenge is the prevalence of tokenism, where organizations may superficially include diverse voices without genuinely valuing their contributions. This can lead to a lack of trust within the community and diminish the effectiveness of advocacy efforts. To combat this, it is essential for LGBTQ organizations to engage in meaningful dialogue with marginalized groups and ensure their representation is authentic and impactful.

## Examples of Celebrating Diversity

Celebrating diversity within the LGBTQ community can take many forms. One prominent example is the annual Pride Month celebrations, which honor the history and contributions of LGBTQ individuals. Events such as parades, festivals, and educational workshops not only raise awareness but also foster a sense of belonging. For instance, the Sydney Gay and Lesbian Mardi Gras has evolved from a protest to a celebration that showcases the rich tapestry of LGBTQ identities.

Moreover, organizations like GLAAD (Gay & Lesbian Alliance Against Defamation) actively work to improve media representation of diverse LGBTQ individuals. By promoting stories that reflect the experiences of various identities, GLAAD helps to combat stereotypes and foster understanding within the broader society.

## Building Inclusive Spaces

Creating inclusive spaces requires intentionality and commitment. One effective approach is the implementation of diversity training programs within organizations. These programs educate staff and volunteers about the importance of inclusivity and equip them with the tools to create welcoming environments. For example, the Trevor Project, which focuses on crisis intervention for LGBTQ youth, emphasizes the importance of training their volunteers to understand the unique challenges faced by LGBTQ individuals, particularly those from marginalized backgrounds.

Additionally, fostering allyship is crucial in building inclusive communities. Allies can play a vital role in amplifying the voices of marginalized groups and advocating for their rights. Initiatives such as ally training workshops can empower individuals to become effective allies, creating a ripple effect of inclusivity throughout the community.

## Conclusion

In conclusion, celebrating diversity and building inclusivity are essential components of the LGBTQ rights movement. By understanding the theoretical foundations of social identity and intersectionality, addressing the challenges of marginalization and tokenism, and actively promoting diverse representation, the community can work towards a more inclusive future. As Sally Rugg exemplifies through her advocacy, embracing diversity is not just a goal; it is a necessity for the progress of the LGBTQ movement and society as a whole. By fostering environments where all identities are celebrated, we pave the way for a brighter, more equitable future for everyone.

# Chapter Two: The Rise of Sally Rugg

## Section One: Advocacy and activism

### Finding her voice

In the journey of any activist, the process of finding one's voice is both a personal and a political endeavor. For Sally Rugg, this journey was marked by the convergence of her experiences as a queer individual and her burgeoning awareness of social justice issues. It began in her formative years, where the intersectionality of her identity played a critical role in shaping her perspective on activism.

Sally's early encounters with homophobia and discrimination ignited a fire within her that demanded expression. The first step in her journey was acknowledging her own narrative. According to [?], "Life-transforming ideas have always come to me through the voices of others." Thus, Sally sought out the voices of those who had come before her, learning from their struggles and triumphs. She immersed herself in literature, documentaries, and community discussions, which helped her articulate the complexities of her identity and the injustices faced by the LGBTQ community.

$$\text{Voice} = \text{Identity} + \text{Experience} + \text{Activism} \tag{9}$$

This equation illustrates that finding one's voice is not a singular event but a synthesis of various elements. Sally's identity as a queer woman, her personal experiences with discrimination, and her engagement with activism coalesced to create a powerful voice that resonated with many.

As she navigated the challenges of coming out, she began to understand the importance of representation. The absence of queer voices in mainstream narratives further fueled her resolve to speak out. She recognized that silence perpetuates oppression, and thus, she committed herself to becoming a vocal advocate for LGBTQ rights. This commitment was not without its challenges; she faced internalized fears and societal pressures that often sought to silence her.

Sally's breakthrough moment came when she participated in a local Pride march. The energy of the crowd, the vibrancy of the flags, and the camaraderie among participants were electrifying. It was here that she felt the weight of collective voices uniting for a common cause. This experience was pivotal, as it allowed her to understand the power of community in amplifying individual voices. As she later stated in an interview, "When we stand together, our voices become a chorus that can no longer be ignored."

$$\text{Collective Voice} = \sum_{i=1}^{n} \text{Individual Voices} \qquad (10)$$

This equation emphasizes the idea that the strength of activism lies in its collective nature. Each individual voice contributes to a larger narrative that can challenge societal norms and demand change. Inspired by this realization, Sally began to seek out opportunities to express her views publicly.

Her initial forays into public speaking were met with trepidation. The fear of backlash loomed large, but she found solace in the supportive LGBTQ community that surrounded her. The encouragement from peers and mentors provided her with the confidence to step onto platforms where her voice could be heard. She began sharing her story at local events, schools, and community centers, emphasizing the importance of authenticity in activism.

Theoretical frameworks such as [?]'s concept of critical consciousness underscore the significance of personal narratives in the fight for social justice. By sharing her experiences, Sally not only found her voice but also empowered others to do the same. She understood that storytelling is a powerful tool for advocacy, capable of fostering empathy and understanding among diverse audiences.

As she honed her public speaking skills, Sally also recognized the importance of strategic communication. Effective activism requires the ability to convey messages clearly and persuasively. She studied the art of rhetoric, learning to craft messages that resonate emotionally while also being grounded in factual evidence. This dual approach enabled her to connect with audiences on multiple levels, whether they were allies or adversaries.

Sally's journey of finding her voice culminated in her role as a spokesperson for the Marriage Equality Campaign. Her speeches became rallying cries for change, filled with passion and urgency. She articulated the struggles of LGBTQ individuals with a clarity that moved people to action. One of her most memorable quotes during a rally encapsulated her ethos: "Love is love, and it deserves to be celebrated, not just tolerated."

In summary, the process of finding her voice was a transformative experience for Sally Rugg. It involved a deep exploration of her identity, a commitment to sharing her story, and the development of skills that would allow her to advocate effectively for LGBTQ rights. By embracing her narrative and amplifying the voices of others, she not only carved out a space for herself in the activist landscape but also inspired countless others to join her in the fight for equality.

## Joining LGBTQ organizations

Sally Rugg's journey into activism took a significant turn when she began to engage with LGBTQ organizations. This decision was not merely a step towards personal advocacy but a pivotal moment that would shape her identity as a leader in the movement for LGBTQ rights in Australia. Joining these organizations provided Sally with a platform to amplify her voice and connect with others who shared her passion for change.

### The Importance of Community

The LGBTQ community has long been characterized by its resilience and solidarity in the face of adversity. Research in social psychology highlights the importance of group identity in fostering a sense of belonging and support among marginalized individuals [1]. For Sally, joining LGBTQ organizations was a way to forge connections with like-minded individuals who understood her struggles and aspirations.

Through these organizations, she found a sense of community that was essential for her personal growth. As she interacted with other activists, Sally learned about the historical context of LGBTQ rights in Australia and the ongoing challenges faced by the community. This knowledge equipped her with the necessary tools to navigate the complex landscape of activism.

### Building Skills and Knowledge

Sally's involvement with LGBTQ organizations provided her with invaluable training and resources. Many organizations offer workshops, mentorship programs, and resources that help individuals develop skills essential for effective advocacy [2]. For instance, Sally participated in public speaking workshops that enhanced her ability to communicate her message effectively.

Moreover, she gained insights into the legislative process and advocacy strategies, which were crucial for her later work in the Marriage Equality Campaign. The theoretical framework of social movement theory emphasizes the importance of resource mobilization, suggesting that access to information and skills is vital for the success of social movements [3].

## Contributing to Collective Action

Joining LGBTQ organizations allowed Sally to contribute to collective action initiatives that aimed to address systemic discrimination and promote equality. One of the primary challenges faced by these organizations is the fragmentation of the LGBTQ movement, which can dilute efforts and resources. However, Sally's participation in various coalitions helped bridge gaps between different factions within the movement, fostering collaboration and unity.

For example, during her time with the Australian Marriage Equality (AME) organization, Sally played a crucial role in coordinating campaigns that brought together diverse LGBTQ groups. This collective action not only amplified their voices but also demonstrated the power of solidarity in the fight for marriage equality. The success of such campaigns is often attributed to the ability of organizations to mobilize resources and people effectively [4].

## Facing Challenges and Resistance

While joining LGBTQ organizations provided Sally with numerous opportunities, it was not without its challenges. Activists often encounter resistance from both societal norms and within their own organizations. For instance, Sally faced pushback from individuals who held more conservative views on LGBTQ rights, which sometimes manifested as hostility during public events and discussions.

Additionally, internal conflicts within organizations can arise, particularly regarding strategy and priorities. Navigating these challenges required Sally to develop strong conflict resolution skills and a commitment to inclusivity. The concept of intersectionality, introduced by Kimberlé Crenshaw, emphasizes the need to consider how various forms of discrimination intersect, which became a guiding principle in Sally's approach to activism [5].

## Impact of Joining LGBTQ Organizations

Sally's decision to join LGBTQ organizations marked the beginning of her transformation into a prominent activist. The connections she made and the skills she developed laid the foundation for her future endeavors. Through her work, she not only advocated for marriage equality but also addressed broader issues affecting the LGBTQ community, such as mental health support and anti-discrimination legislation.

The impact of joining these organizations extended beyond her personal journey; it contributed to a larger movement that sought to challenge societal norms and promote acceptance. Sally's story is a testament to the power of community and the importance of collective action in effecting change.

In conclusion, Sally Rugg's involvement with LGBTQ organizations was a critical step in her journey as an activist. It provided her with the community, skills, and opportunities necessary to become a leading voice in the fight for LGBTQ rights in Australia. By embracing the challenges and harnessing the power of collective action, Sally exemplified the transformative potential of joining forces with others in the pursuit of equality.

# Bibliography

[1] Tajfel, H. (1986). *Social Identity and Intergroup Relations*. Cambridge University Press.

[2] Meyer, D. S. (2008). *The Politics of Protest: Social Movements in America*. Oxford University Press.

[3] Tilly, C. (2004). *Social Movements, 1768-2004*. Paradigm Publishers.

[4] McAdam, D. (1982). *Political Process and the Development of Black Insurgency, 1930-1970*. University of Chicago Press.

[5] Crenshaw, K. (1989). Demarginalizing the Intersection of Race and Sex: A Black Feminist Critique of Antidiscrimination Doctrine, Feminist Theory and Antiracist Politics. *University of Chicago Legal Forum*, 1989(1), 139-167.

## Co-founding the Marriage Equality Campaign

In the heart of Australia's LGBTQ rights movement, Sally Rugg emerged as a pivotal figure in the co-founding of the Marriage Equality Campaign. This initiative was not merely a political endeavor; it was a profound statement of love, dignity, and equality. The campaign sought to challenge the long-standing legal barriers that prevented same-sex couples from enjoying the same marital rights as their heterosexual counterparts.

## Theoretical Framework

At its core, the Marriage Equality Campaign was grounded in several key theoretical frameworks. The most prominent among these was the theory of social justice, which posits that all individuals deserve equitable treatment and access to rights regardless of their sexual orientation. John Rawls' principles of justice emphasize fairness and equality, suggesting that any societal structure should be designed to benefit the least advantaged. In the context of marriage equality, this meant advocating for the inclusion of LGBTQ individuals in the institution of marriage, which has historically been a cornerstone of societal recognition and legitimacy.

Another critical theoretical underpinning was the concept of intersectionality, coined by Kimberlé Crenshaw. This theory highlights how various forms of discrimination—such as those based on race, gender, and sexual orientation—intersect to create unique experiences of oppression. The campaign sought to address not only the rights of same-sex couples but also the broader implications for LGBTQ individuals from diverse backgrounds, ensuring that the movement was inclusive and representative of all voices.

## Challenges Faced

The journey to co-founding the Marriage Equality Campaign was fraught with challenges. One of the primary obstacles was the entrenched societal norms that upheld heteronormativity—the assumption that heterosexual relationships are the default or "normal" form of human connection. This bias was reflected in the legal framework, which explicitly defined marriage as a union between a man and a woman.

Furthermore, the campaign faced significant opposition from various religious and conservative groups who argued that marriage should be preserved as a traditional institution. These groups leveraged media platforms to propagate misinformation and fear, often framing the issue as a threat to family values. The rhetoric surrounding the campaign was emotionally charged, and the stakes were high, as LGBTQ individuals were often portrayed as seeking to undermine societal foundations.

## Building the Campaign

In response to these challenges, Sally Rugg and her co-founders took a strategic approach to build the Marriage Equality Campaign. They recognized the necessity of grassroots mobilization and community engagement. This involved organizing rallies, community forums, and educational workshops aimed at raising awareness about the importance of marriage equality.

One of the campaign's most notable strategies was the use of storytelling as a powerful tool for advocacy. By sharing personal narratives of love, commitment, and the struggles faced by same-sex couples, the campaign humanized the issue. These stories resonated with the public, fostering empathy and understanding. The campaign also utilized social media platforms to amplify these narratives, reaching a broader audience and creating a sense of solidarity among supporters.

## Legislative Advocacy

The Marriage Equality Campaign was not just about raising awareness; it was also a concerted effort to influence legislative change. Rugg and her team engaged with policymakers, presenting data and research that illustrated the positive societal impacts of marriage equality. They highlighted studies showing that marriage equality contributes to the mental health and well-being of LGBTQ individuals, leading to a more inclusive and harmonious society.

The campaign also sought to mobilize allies within the political sphere. By building coalitions with sympathetic lawmakers and organizations, they were able to create a united front advocating for legislative reform. This collaborative approach was instrumental in shifting the political landscape, as more politicians began to publicly support marriage equality.

## Successes and Impact

The culmination of these efforts was a significant victory for the Marriage Equality Campaign when Australia legalized same-sex marriage in December 2017. This landmark decision was a testament to the power of grassroots activism and the relentless pursuit of justice. Sally Rugg's role in co-founding the campaign not only changed the legal landscape for LGBTQ individuals in Australia but also inspired a generation of activists around the world.

The success of the campaign had far-reaching implications, reinforcing the notion that love knows no bounds and that equality is a fundamental human right. It demonstrated the effectiveness of collective action in challenging systemic discrimination and paved the way for further advancements in LGBTQ rights.

## Conclusion

In conclusion, the co-founding of the Marriage Equality Campaign by Sally Rugg marked a significant turning point in Australia's LGBTQ rights movement. Through a combination of theoretical frameworks, grassroots mobilization, and strategic advocacy, the campaign overcame formidable challenges to achieve a historic victory. This chapter of Rugg's life not only solidified her legacy as a leader in the fight for equality but also served as a beacon of hope for LGBTQ individuals everywhere, reminding them that change is possible when voices unite for justice.

## Impactful speeches and public appearances

Sally Rugg's journey as an activist is punctuated by her powerful speeches and public appearances, which have not only inspired countless individuals but also catalyzed significant changes in societal attitudes towards LGBTQ rights. Her ability to articulate the struggles and aspirations of the LGBTQ community has made her a formidable figure in the fight for equality.

## The Power of Speech

Research in communication theory, particularly the *Rhetorical Situation* as proposed by Lloyd Bitzer, emphasizes that effective communication is contingent upon the context in which it occurs. Rugg's speeches often address the exigence of the moment—whether it be a rally for marriage equality or a response to a discriminatory policy—allowing her to resonate deeply with her audience.

$$\text{Rhetorical Effectiveness} = f(\text{Audience Engagement, Message Clarity, Emotional Ap}$$
$$(11)$$

In this equation, the effectiveness of Rugg's rhetoric can be seen as a function of how well she engages her audience, the clarity of her message, and the emotional resonance of her delivery.

## Key Speeches

One of Rugg's most notable speeches was delivered at the *Marriage Equality Rally* in Melbourne in 2017. Here, she addressed the crowd with fervor, stating:

> "We are not asking for special treatment. We are demanding equal rights. Love is love, and it knows no bounds. It's time our laws reflect the values we hold dear as a society."

This moment not only galvanized the audience but also garnered significant media attention, amplifying her message beyond the immediate crowd. The speech exemplified her ability to frame LGBTQ rights as a fundamental human issue, a strategy rooted in the *Framing Theory* which posits that the way information is presented influences public perception and opinion.

## Media Engagement

Rugg's public appearances extend beyond rallies; she has been a prominent figure in various media outlets, including television interviews and podcasts. In a notable interview on *The Project*, she discussed the implications of the Australian government's stance on LGBTQ rights, highlighting the psychological impact of discrimination on young queer individuals.

> "When the government tells you that your love is not valid, it echoes in the hearts of our youth. It sends a message that they are less than, and that is a dangerous narrative to perpetuate."

This statement not only engaged viewers but also prompted discussions around mental health within the LGBTQ community, showcasing Rugg's ability to connect personal narratives with broader societal issues.

## Confronting Challenges in Public Speaking

Despite her success, Rugg has faced challenges in her public speaking engagements. The backlash against her views has often manifested in hate speech and threats, particularly on social media platforms. However, her resilience shines through in her ability to address these challenges head-on. For instance, during a particularly hostile interview, she remarked:

> "If they think that their hate will silence me, they are sorely mistaken. My voice is louder than their hate, and I will continue to fight for our rights."

This response not only deflected the negativity but also reinforced her commitment to advocacy, embodying the principles of *Cognitive Dissonance Theory*, where individuals strive for internal consistency in their beliefs and actions.

## Legacy of Influence

Rugg's impactful speeches and public appearances have left an indelible mark on the LGBTQ rights movement in Australia. Her ability to mobilize support and foster dialogue around complex issues has inspired a new generation of activists. As she once said:

> "We are the change we seek. Every voice matters, and together, we can create a future where love knows no bounds."

In conclusion, Sally Rugg's speeches and public engagements serve as a testament to the power of voice in activism. By leveraging her platform, she has not only advocated for policy changes but has also cultivated a sense of community and empowerment among LGBTQ individuals. Her legacy will undoubtedly continue to inspire and motivate future generations in the ongoing fight for equality.

## Influencing policy and legislative change

Sally Rugg's impact on policy and legislative change in Australia is a testament to the power of grassroots activism combined with strategic advocacy. As she navigated the complex landscape of LGBTQ rights, she utilized a variety of approaches to influence lawmakers and shift public opinion towards acceptance and equality.

### Theoretical Framework

To understand Sally's influence, we can apply the Advocacy Coalition Framework (ACF), which posits that policy change occurs through the interaction of various coalitions of actors who share a set of beliefs. In the context of LGBTQ rights, Rugg's coalition included activists, legal experts, and supportive politicians who worked together to promote marriage equality and anti-discrimination laws. This collaboration was crucial in shaping the legislative agenda and mobilizing public support.

$$\text{Policy Change} = f(\text{Coalition Strength}, \text{Public Support}, \text{Political Opportunity}) \tag{12}$$

Where: - Coalition Strength refers to the unity and resources of advocacy groups. - Public Support is the level of societal backing for LGBTQ rights. - Political Opportunity reflects the openness of political institutions to new ideas.

### Strategic Approaches

Rugg's strategy involved several key components:

1. **Building Coalitions**: By co-founding the Marriage Equality Campaign, Rugg united various LGBTQ organizations, legal advocates, and allies to create a formidable coalition. This coalition was instrumental in amplifying voices and consolidating resources, making a compelling case for change.

2. **Lobbying Efforts**: Rugg and her colleagues engaged in targeted lobbying of politicians, educating them on the importance of marriage equality and the impact of discrimination on LGBTQ individuals. This involved personal stories,

data-driven arguments, and the mobilization of constituents to pressure their representatives.

3. **Public Campaigns**: Utilizing social media and traditional media platforms, Rugg spearheaded campaigns that raised awareness and generated public support for LGBTQ rights. Campaigns such as "Equality for All" featured compelling narratives that humanized the issue, making it relatable to a broader audience.

## Case Studies

One of the most significant achievements during Rugg's advocacy was the successful push for marriage equality in Australia, culminating in the 2017 postal survey. This survey, which asked Australians whether they supported changing the law to allow same-sex couples to marry, was a pivotal moment in the movement. Rugg played a crucial role in mobilizing support for the "Yes" campaign, organizing rallies, and leveraging social media to reach younger voters.

$$\text{Support for Marriage Equality} = \text{Awareness} + \text{Personal Stories} + \text{Visibility} \quad (13)$$

Where: - Awareness refers to the public's understanding of LGBTQ issues. - Personal Stories highlight the lived experiences of LGBTQ individuals. - Visibility denotes the representation of LGBTQ people in media and politics.

The success of the campaign was reflected in the overwhelming response to the postal survey, with approximately 61.6% voting in favor of marriage equality. This result not only influenced the legislative process but also signaled a significant shift in public attitudes toward LGBTQ rights.

## Challenges Faced

Despite these successes, Rugg and her coalition faced numerous challenges. Opposition from conservative groups and political factions resistant to change posed significant hurdles. The discourse around marriage equality often included misinformation and fear-mongering, which Rugg and her allies had to counteract through education and advocacy.

Moreover, navigating the political landscape required patience and resilience. Legislative change is often slow and fraught with setbacks. Rugg's ability to maintain momentum and keep the coalition united was critical during these challenging times.

## Conclusion

Sally Rugg's influence on policy and legislative change in Australia serves as a powerful example of how activism can lead to tangible results. Through coalition-building, strategic lobbying, and effective public campaigns, she not only advanced LGBTQ rights but also inspired a generation of activists to continue the fight for equality. The lessons learned from her journey underscore the importance of persistence, collaboration, and the need for a multifaceted approach to advocacy.

In summary, Rugg's work exemplifies how theory and practice intertwine in the realm of social change, demonstrating that with the right strategies and a committed coalition, significant legislative victories can be achieved.

# Section Two: Media and public figure

## Becoming a recognizable face

In the world of activism, visibility can be both a powerful tool and a double-edged sword. For Sally Rugg, the journey to becoming a recognizable face in LGBTQ activism was marked by a blend of courage, strategy, and the relentless pursuit of justice. As she emerged from the shadows of her own struggles, she transformed into a beacon of hope for many, embodying the spirit of a movement that demanded equality and recognition.

## The Power of Visibility

The concept of visibility in activism is rooted in the idea that representation matters. When individuals see themselves reflected in leadership roles, it fosters a sense of belonging and empowerment. Sally Rugg understood this dynamic intimately. As she began to share her story publicly, she not only raised awareness about the challenges faced by LGBTQ individuals but also humanized the statistics that often dominate discussions around queer rights.

Visibility, however, comes with its own set of challenges. The more recognizable Sally became, the more scrutiny she faced. This phenomenon is well-documented in social psychology, where the *social comparison theory* posits that individuals determine their own social and personal worth based on how they stack up against others. For Sally, this meant navigating the complexities of public perception while remaining true to her mission.

## Media Engagement and Strategy

To amplify her message, Sally strategically engaged with various media platforms. She recognized that traditional media outlets, such as newspapers and television, played a crucial role in shaping public opinion. Her early interviews were not just about sharing her experiences; they were opportunities to educate the public about LGBTQ issues. For instance, during a pivotal interview with a national broadcaster, she articulated the emotional and psychological toll of discrimination, effectively putting a human face to the statistics surrounding LGBTQ youth suicide rates.

Moreover, Sally's presence on social media platforms further solidified her status as a recognizable figure. In a digital age where information spreads rapidly, she utilized platforms like Twitter and Instagram to engage directly with her audience. This approach not only allowed her to share her advocacy work but also to foster a community of supporters who could amplify her message. The equation for successful social media engagement can be simplified as:

$$E = R \cdot (C + I)$$

Where $E$ is engagement, $R$ is reach, $C$ is content quality, and $I$ is interaction. Sally's ability to craft compelling narratives while encouraging dialogue exemplified this formula.

## Navigating Public Scrutiny

As her visibility grew, so did the scrutiny. Public figures often face backlash, and Sally was no exception. The rise of social media has amplified this phenomenon, creating an environment where criticism can spread like wildfire. Sally's experience with online hate speech and personal attacks illustrates the darker side of visibility. The psychological impact of such scrutiny can lead to what is known as *imposter syndrome*, where individuals doubt their accomplishments and fear being exposed as a "fraud."

To combat these challenges, Sally leaned into her support network. Engaging with fellow activists and mental health professionals provided her with the tools to cope with adversity. The importance of community support in activism cannot be overstated; it serves as a buffer against the emotional toll of public life. Research indicates that social support can significantly mitigate the effects of stress, promoting resilience in individuals facing external pressures.

## The Role of Authenticity

Throughout her journey, authenticity emerged as a cornerstone of Sally's public persona. In a world where activists can be commodified or misrepresented, staying true to oneself is vital. Sally's willingness to share her personal story of coming out and the struggles she faced resonated with many. This authenticity not only endeared her to supporters but also positioned her as a relatable figure in a landscape often dominated by polished narratives.

The theory of *authentic leadership* posits that leaders who remain true to their values and beliefs foster trust and loyalty among their followers. Sally's approach exemplified this theory; her transparency about her challenges and triumphs inspired others to embrace their own identities and engage in activism.

## Conclusion

Sally Rugg's ascent to becoming a recognizable face in LGBTQ activism is a testament to the power of visibility, strategic media engagement, and authenticity. While the path was fraught with challenges, her resilience and commitment to her cause have left an indelible mark on the movement. As she continues to navigate the complexities of public life, her journey serves as a reminder that visibility is not just about being seen; it's about using that visibility to effect real change in the world.

## TV and radio interviews

In the landscape of modern activism, media presence plays a pivotal role in shaping public perception and advancing causes. For Sally Rugg, her journey as an LGBTQ activist was significantly amplified through her appearances on television and radio, where she adeptly navigated the complexities of media engagement to further the rights and visibility of the LGBTQ community.

## The Power of Media

Television and radio serve as powerful platforms for activists to communicate their messages, engage with broader audiences, and influence public discourse. According to [?], media acts as a conduit for social change, providing visibility to marginalized voices and issues. This visibility is essential for movements like LGBTQ rights, where representation can lead to greater acceptance and understanding.

## Early Appearances

Sally's initial forays into the media spotlight began with local radio stations, where she discussed her experiences and the challenges faced by the LGBTQ community. These interviews were critical in establishing her as a relatable figure, giving her the opportunity to share personal narratives that resonated with listeners. A pivotal moment occurred during an interview on *ABC Radio*, where she articulated the emotional toll of discrimination, stating:

> "The pain of being marginalized is not just a statistic; it's a lived experience that many carry in silence. By sharing my story, I hope to break that silence."

This powerful narrative not only humanized the struggle but also encouraged others to share their stories, fostering a sense of community.

## Television Engagements

As Sally's profile grew, so did her opportunities for television appearances. She became a recognizable face on programs such as *The Project* and *Q&A*, where she tackled pressing issues like marriage equality and anti-discrimination laws. These platforms allowed her to reach a diverse audience, including those who may not have been previously engaged in LGBTQ issues.

During her appearance on *The Project*, Sally addressed the misconceptions surrounding LGBTQ relationships, asserting:

> "Love is love, and it transcends gender. We all deserve the right to marry the person we love, regardless of who they are."

This statement not only challenged prevailing stereotypes but also appealed to the emotions of viewers, making the case for marriage equality more accessible.

## Navigating Public Scrutiny

With increased visibility came public scrutiny. Sally faced backlash from conservative groups and individuals opposed to LGBTQ rights. In an interview on *Sky News*, she was confronted with challenging questions that sought to undermine her stance. Instead of shying away from confrontation, Sally used these moments to articulate her beliefs more passionately. She stated:

"Disagreement is part of democracy, but it should never justify discrimination. We must engage in respectful dialogue, but we must also stand firm in our rights."

Her ability to maintain composure and articulate her points amidst criticism showcased her strength as a leader and advocate.

## Social Media Synergy

Sally's media presence extended beyond traditional platforms into the realm of social media. Her strategic use of platforms like Twitter and Instagram complemented her television and radio appearances, allowing her to engage with younger audiences who consume news differently. For instance, after a compelling interview, she often took to Twitter to expand on her points, using hashtags like #LoveIsLove and #EqualityNow to mobilize support.

The synergy between traditional media and social media is well-documented. According to [?], social media not only amplifies messages but also fosters community engagement. Sally's adeptness at using these platforms helped her build a robust support network, turning viewers into active participants in the LGBTQ rights movement.

## Impact on Public Discourse

Sally Rugg's media appearances have undeniably shifted public discourse surrounding LGBTQ rights in Australia. By consistently presenting herself as an articulate and passionate advocate, she has contributed to a broader understanding of LGBTQ issues. Her interviews have served as educational moments, breaking down complex legal and social issues into digestible narratives for the public.

For instance, her discussion on the implications of the *Marriage Amendment (Definition and Religious Freedoms) Act 2017* on LGBTQ families highlighted the ongoing challenges faced by the community, prompting conversations that extended beyond the media into homes and workplaces.

## Conclusion

In summary, Sally Rugg's television and radio interviews have been instrumental in her journey as an activist. Through these platforms, she has not only shared her story but has also educated the public, challenged misconceptions, and advocated for change. As the media landscape continues to evolve, the role of activists like Sally remains crucial in driving conversations that lead to social progress and equality.

# Navigating public scrutiny

Navigating public scrutiny is a critical aspect of being a public figure, especially for LGBTQ activists like Sally Rugg. The intersection of activism and public life often subjects individuals to intense examination, both positive and negative. This scrutiny can manifest through media coverage, public opinion, and the ever-present gaze of social media platforms. Understanding how to manage this scrutiny is essential for maintaining one's mental health, effectiveness as an advocate, and the overall mission of promoting LGBTQ rights.

## The Nature of Public Scrutiny

Public scrutiny can be understood as the critical observation and evaluation of an individual's actions, beliefs, and character by the public. This phenomenon is not new; however, the rise of social media has amplified its reach and intensity. For LGBTQ activists, this scrutiny can be particularly harsh due to existing societal prejudices and the politicization of LGBTQ issues.

**Media Representation**    Media plays a significant role in shaping public perception. Activists like Sally Rugg often find themselves at the center of media narratives that can either bolster or undermine their message. For instance, during her advocacy for marriage equality, Rugg was frequently portrayed in various lights—heroic in some outlets and controversial in others. This duality underscores the importance of understanding media dynamics and working with journalists to frame narratives positively.

## Coping Mechanisms

To navigate public scrutiny effectively, activists need to develop coping mechanisms. These can include:

- **Building a Support Network:** Establishing a strong support system of friends, family, and fellow activists can provide emotional resilience. This network can serve as a buffer against negative public sentiment and provide constructive feedback.

- **Media Training:** Engaging in media training can equip activists with the skills to handle interviews, press conferences, and public appearances. Understanding how to communicate effectively under pressure can mitigate the impact of scrutiny.

+ **Mental Health Resources:** Accessing mental health resources is crucial for coping with the stress of public life. Therapy or counseling can help activists process their experiences and develop strategies for resilience.

## Examples of Navigating Scrutiny

Sally Rugg's journey illustrates the complexities of navigating public scrutiny. During her campaign for marriage equality, she faced backlash from conservative groups and individuals who opposed her views. One notable incident involved a social media campaign that targeted her with hate speech and personal attacks. Rather than retreating, Rugg utilized these experiences to fuel her activism, emphasizing the importance of resilience in the face of adversity.

**Public Engagement**    Rugg also learned to engage with her critics constructively. By addressing misconceptions and providing factual information about LGBTQ rights, she transformed negative scrutiny into opportunities for education. For example, during a televised debate, she confronted a critic with statistics highlighting the positive societal impacts of marriage equality, effectively reframing the conversation.

## The Role of Social Media

Social media platforms serve as double-edged swords for activists. While they offer a space for advocacy and community building, they also expose individuals to public scrutiny on an unprecedented scale. Rugg's strategic use of platforms like Twitter and Instagram allowed her to connect with supporters, share her message, and counteract negative narratives in real-time.

**Digital Resilience**    Developing digital resilience is crucial for activists navigating online scrutiny. This includes:

+ **Curating Content:** Activists must be mindful of the content they share and how it may be perceived. Rugg often curated her posts to highlight positive stories and achievements within the LGBTQ community, reinforcing a narrative of hope and progress.

+ **Engaging with Supporters:** Actively engaging with supportive comments and messages can help counterbalance negative feedback. Rugg often took time to respond to supporters, creating a sense of community and solidarity.

⁕ **Setting Boundaries:** Knowing when to disengage from toxic discussions is vital. Rugg learned to set boundaries around her online presence, prioritizing her mental health over engaging with trolls or detractors.

## Conclusion

In conclusion, navigating public scrutiny is an integral part of Sally Rugg's journey as an LGBTQ activist. By understanding the nature of scrutiny, developing effective coping mechanisms, and utilizing social media strategically, Rugg has managed to turn challenges into opportunities for growth and advocacy. Her experiences underscore the importance of resilience, support, and education in the face of public scrutiny, serving as a valuable lesson for aspiring activists. The ability to navigate this scrutiny not only enhances personal well-being but also strengthens the broader movement for LGBTQ rights, ensuring that the fight for equality continues to thrive amidst challenges.

## Social media presence and engagement

In the digital age, social media has become an indispensable tool for activists, offering a platform to amplify their voices, mobilize support, and engage with the public. For Sally Rugg, her social media presence was not just a byproduct of her activism; it was a strategic element of her advocacy that reshaped how LGBTQ issues were communicated and perceived in Australia.

### The Importance of Social Media in Activism

Social media platforms such as Twitter, Instagram, and Facebook have revolutionized the landscape of activism. According to [?], social media facilitates the rapid dissemination of information, allowing activists to reach a global audience instantaneously. This capability is particularly crucial for marginalized communities, which often struggle to have their voices heard in mainstream media.

Sally Rugg harnessed this power effectively. Her Twitter account became a hub for rallying support, sharing personal stories, and disseminating critical information about LGBTQ rights. The immediacy of social media allowed her to respond quickly to unfolding events, such as legislative debates or instances of discrimination, providing real-time updates and mobilizing her followers to take action.

## Engagement Strategies

Rugg employed several engagement strategies to cultivate a robust online community. One of the most effective was her use of storytelling. By sharing her own experiences, Rugg humanized the issues at stake, making them relatable to a broader audience. As highlighted by [?], personal narratives can foster empathy and understanding, bridging the gap between activists and the general public.

Moreover, Rugg frequently utilized hashtags to unify conversations around specific topics. For instance, during the campaign for marriage equality, she promoted hashtags like #MarriageEquality and #LoveIsLove, which helped galvanize support and create a sense of solidarity among followers. This tactic aligns with the findings of [?], who noted that hashtags can serve as rallying points for collective action.

## Challenges of Social Media Engagement

Despite its advantages, social media engagement is fraught with challenges. Rugg faced significant backlash and hate speech online, particularly from opponents of LGBTQ rights. According to [?], online harassment is a pervasive issue for activists, often leading to emotional distress and burnout. Rugg's ability to navigate this hostile environment was critical to her resilience as an activist.

To combat negativity, Rugg adopted a policy of selective engagement. She chose to amplify positive messages and constructive criticism while ignoring or blocking overtly hostile comments. This approach not only protected her mental health but also reinforced a positive narrative around her activism. As noted by [?], maintaining a positive online presence can enhance an activist's credibility and influence.

## Impact on Public Perception

Rugg's social media presence significantly influenced public perception of LGBTQ issues in Australia. Her posts often went viral, reaching audiences beyond her immediate followers and sparking conversations in mainstream media. Research by [?] indicates that social media can shape public discourse, particularly on contentious issues like marriage equality.

For example, during the lead-up to the postal survey on marriage equality in 2017, Rugg's social media campaign played a pivotal role in shaping the narrative. She shared statistics, personal stories, and calls to action that resonated with the public, ultimately contributing to the overwhelming support for marriage equality. This phenomenon is supported by [?], who found that social media campaigns can significantly sway public opinion when executed effectively.

## Conclusion

In conclusion, Sally Rugg's social media presence and engagement were integral to her role as an LGBTQ activist. By leveraging the power of storytelling, strategic hashtag use, and a positive online persona, she was able to mobilize support and influence public perception. However, she also faced the harsh realities of online activism, navigating hate speech and backlash with resilience and grace. Rugg's experience underscores the dual-edged nature of social media in activism—while it offers unprecedented opportunities for engagement and outreach, it also presents significant challenges that activists must confront. As Rugg continues her journey, her adept use of social media serves as a blueprint for future activists seeking to make a difference in the digital age.

# Balancing personal and professional life

In the world of activism, particularly within the LGBTQ community, the line between personal and professional life often blurs. For Sally Rugg, this balance was not just a matter of time management; it was a continuous negotiation of identity, purpose, and emotional well-being. The challenges she faced in maintaining this equilibrium reflect broader themes in activism, where the personal is inherently political.

## Theoretical Framework

The concept of work-life balance has been extensively studied, with theories such as the **Boundary Theory** (Nippert-Eng, 1996) suggesting that individuals create and manage boundaries between their work and personal lives. This theory posits that these boundaries can be flexible or rigid, depending on the individual's circumstances and choices. For activists like Rugg, the boundaries are often permeable, as their personal identities are deeply intertwined with their professional missions.

## Challenges Faced

Sally encountered several challenges in her quest to balance her personal and professional life:

- **Emotional Labor:** Activism demands a significant amount of emotional investment. Rugg often found herself navigating the emotional toll of advocating for marginalized communities while managing her own mental health. This emotional labor can lead to burnout if not properly managed.

+ **Public Scrutiny:** As a public figure, Rugg faced intense scrutiny, which can complicate personal relationships. The pressure to maintain a public persona while dealing with personal struggles can create a sense of isolation. For instance, during her advocacy for marriage equality, the backlash she faced from opponents often seeped into her personal life, affecting her relationships with friends and family.

+ **Time Management:** Balancing the demands of activism with personal commitments required exceptional time management skills. Rugg often had to prioritize her activism over personal time, leading to conflicts and feelings of guilt. The challenge lies in recognizing that self-care is not a luxury but a necessity for sustained activism.

## Strategies for Balance

To navigate these challenges, Rugg adopted several strategies that allowed her to maintain a semblance of balance:

+ **Setting Boundaries:** Rugg learned the importance of setting clear boundaries between her work and personal life. This included designating specific times for activism and ensuring she had time for herself, family, and friends.

+ **Mindfulness and Self-Care:** Engaging in mindfulness practices helped Rugg manage stress and maintain her mental health. Activities such as meditation, exercise, and hobbies provided her with the necessary respite from the demands of her activism.

+ **Support Networks:** Rugg emphasized the importance of surrounding herself with a supportive network of friends and fellow activists. These relationships provided emotional support and understanding, allowing her to share her struggles and triumphs without judgment.

## Examples from Rugg's Life

One notable example of Rugg's struggle to balance her dual roles occurred during the lead-up to the marriage equality vote in Australia. The intense campaigning required her to dedicate long hours to advocacy work, often at the expense of personal time. During this period, she made a conscious effort to schedule regular catch-ups with friends and family, recognizing that these moments were vital for her emotional well-being.

Moreover, Rugg publicly shared her experiences with burnout and the importance of self-care, encouraging other activists to prioritize their mental health. This openness not only humanized her but also fostered a culture of vulnerability and support within the activist community.

## Conclusion

In conclusion, balancing personal and professional life is a complex and ongoing process for activists like Sally Rugg. It requires constant negotiation and adaptation, as well as a commitment to self-care and boundary-setting. Rugg's journey highlights the importance of recognizing that personal well-being is integral to effective activism. By sharing her experiences and strategies, she not only empowers herself but also inspires others to find their own balance in the pursuit of justice and equality.

# Bibliography

[1] Nippert-Eng, C. E. (1996). *Home and Work: Negotiating Boundaries through Everyday Life*. University of Chicago Press.

## Section Three: Confronting challenges

### Dealing with backlash and hate speech

As a prominent figure in the LGBTQ rights movement, Sally Rugg faced significant backlash and hate speech, a reality that many activists encounter in their quest for justice and equality. This section delves into the complexities of dealing with such negative responses, highlighting the psychological impact, theoretical frameworks, and real-world examples that illustrate the challenges faced by activists like Rugg.

### The Nature of Backlash

Backlash against LGBTQ activism often manifests in various forms, including verbal abuse, social media harassment, and organized campaigns aimed at discrediting activists. Theories of social change suggest that backlash is a common reaction to perceived threats against the status quo. According to *The Social Movement Theory*, when marginalized groups advocate for their rights, they challenge existing power structures, prompting defensive reactions from those who feel their privileges are threatened.

For instance, Rugg experienced a surge of hate speech following her public statements advocating for marriage equality. This backlash was not merely personal; it reflected a broader societal resistance to change. Hate speech, as defined by the *International Covenant on Civil and Political Rights*, includes any advocacy of national, racial, or religious hatred that incites discrimination, hostility, or violence. The legal implications of hate speech often complicate the responses of activists, who must navigate the fine line between free expression and the harm caused by such rhetoric.

## Psychological Impact

The psychological toll of experiencing backlash and hate speech can be profound. Activists like Rugg often report feelings of isolation, anxiety, and depression as a result of the hostility directed towards them. According to the *Minority Stress Theory*, individuals from marginalized groups experience chronic stress due to their social stigma, which can lead to mental health challenges.

Rugg's journey illustrates this theory. After receiving numerous threats and derogatory comments on social media, she found herself grappling with self-doubt and fear for her safety. The cumulative effect of such experiences can lead to burnout, which is a significant concern among activists. Research indicates that fostering resilience and coping strategies is crucial for mitigating these effects.

## Coping Mechanisms

To combat the negative effects of backlash, Rugg employed several coping mechanisms. Firstly, she sought support from her community, recognizing the importance of solidarity among LGBTQ individuals. Engaging with supportive networks provided her with a sense of belonging and validation, which is essential for resilience.

Additionally, Rugg utilized social media as a platform not only for advocacy but also for connection. By sharing her experiences and inviting dialogue, she transformed her narrative from one of victimization to empowerment. This approach aligns with the *Empowerment Theory*, which posits that individuals can gain strength through shared experiences and collective action.

## Real-World Examples

One notable instance of backlash occurred during the lead-up to the marriage equality referendum in Australia. Rugg, alongside other activists, faced an onslaught of negative advertisements and public statements from opposition groups. These campaigns often relied on fear tactics, suggesting that marriage equality would undermine traditional family structures. In response, Rugg and her colleagues launched a counter-campaign that emphasized love, equality, and the positive impact of marriage on LGBTQ families.

Moreover, Rugg's experience highlights the role of social media in both perpetuating and combating hate speech. For example, when Rugg was targeted by online trolls, she chose to address the hate directly through public statements that reframed the conversation. By highlighting the absurdity of the hate speech and focusing on the values of love and acceptance, she effectively turned a negative experience into a teachable moment.

## Conclusion

Dealing with backlash and hate speech is an integral part of the activism landscape. For Sally Rugg, the challenges she faced were not merely obstacles but opportunities for growth and solidarity within the LGBTQ community. By employing coping strategies, seeking support, and reframing negative narratives, Rugg exemplified resilience in the face of adversity. Her journey serves as a testament to the power of activism in transforming personal pain into collective progress, ultimately contributing to a more inclusive society.

In conclusion, while the experience of backlash and hate speech can be daunting, it also highlights the ongoing struggle for LGBTQ rights. Activists like Rugg continue to pave the way for future generations, demonstrating that resilience, community, and empowerment are vital in the fight against discrimination and injustice.

## Support from the LGBTQ community

The journey of activism is seldom a solitary one; it is often buoyed by the collective strength of a community. For Sally Rugg, the support she received from the LGBTQ community was not merely a backdrop to her advocacy but a vital lifeline that propelled her forward in the face of adversity. This section delves into the multifaceted support systems that exist within the LGBTQ community and how they played a crucial role in Rugg's activism.

### Community Solidarity

At the heart of LGBTQ activism lies an intrinsic sense of community solidarity. This solidarity manifests in numerous ways, from grassroots organizing to large-scale mobilizations. The LGBTQ community has a long history of coming together to confront challenges, whether they be social, political, or personal. The concept of *collective identity* is essential here, as it fosters a sense of belonging and shared purpose among individuals who have faced similar struggles.

Sally Rugg's involvement in LGBTQ organizations exemplifies this solidarity. By joining forces with groups like the Marriage Equality Campaign, she tapped into a reservoir of shared experiences and collective strength. The campaign itself was a testament to the power of community, bringing together diverse voices to advocate for a common goal: the right to marry for same-sex couples. The camaraderie among activists created a supportive environment where individuals could share their stories, strategies, and resources, thereby amplifying their impact.

## Emotional and Psychological Support

Activism can be emotionally taxing, especially for individuals who face backlash and discrimination. The LGBTQ community provides a critical support network that helps activists navigate these emotional challenges. Research indicates that social support is a significant predictor of resilience among marginalized groups (Cohen & Wills, 1985). This emotional backing can take various forms, including peer support groups, mentorship programs, and informal networks of friends and allies.

Rugg benefited from such support throughout her career. When faced with personal attacks and threats, she found solace in the understanding and encouragement of fellow activists. These connections were not only comforting but also empowering, as they reinforced her commitment to the cause. The LGBTQ community's ability to foster resilience among its members is a vital component of its activism, allowing individuals to persevere despite the odds.

## Mobilization and Collective Action

The LGBTQ community has a rich history of mobilization and collective action, which has been instrumental in advancing rights and achieving legislative victories. Events such as Pride marches and protests serve as powerful demonstrations of unity and purpose. These gatherings not only provide visibility to LGBTQ issues but also create a sense of solidarity among participants.

For Sally Rugg, participating in these events was more than just a symbolic act; it was a strategic move that galvanized support for the Marriage Equality Campaign. The visibility provided by these events helped to shift public perception and put pressure on lawmakers to act. The collective action taken by the LGBTQ community during pivotal moments in history, such as the 2017 marriage equality postal survey, showcased the power of unity in the face of adversity.

## Intersectionality and Inclusivity

Support within the LGBTQ community is not monolithic; it is shaped by various intersecting identities, including race, gender, and socioeconomic status. Understanding this intersectionality is crucial for fostering an inclusive environment that addresses the diverse needs of all community members. Sally

Rugg's activism has often emphasized the importance of inclusivity, advocating for the rights of marginalized groups within the LGBTQ spectrum.

The support from the LGBTQ community extends beyond mere acknowledgment of these intersecting identities; it involves active engagement and advocacy. For instance, Rugg has worked alongside Indigenous LGBTQ activists to ensure that their voices are heard in broader conversations about rights and representation. This commitment to intersectionality enriches the community's activism, making it more robust and representative of the diverse experiences within it.

## Case Studies and Examples

To illustrate the support from the LGBTQ community, we can look at several case studies that highlight this dynamic. One notable example is the Australian Marriage Equality Campaign, where Rugg played a pivotal role. The campaign was characterized by a grassroots approach, with local LGBTQ organizations collaborating to mobilize support. This collaboration exemplified the community's ability to unite for a common cause, leveraging each group's strengths to create a powerful movement.

Another example is the establishment of safe spaces for LGBTQ youth. Organizations such as *Minus18* provide support and resources for young queer individuals, fostering a sense of belonging and community. These initiatives not only offer emotional support but also empower youth to become active participants in advocacy. Rugg's involvement in such initiatives underscores the importance of nurturing the next generation of activists, ensuring that the fight for equality continues.

## Conclusion

In conclusion, the support from the LGBTQ community has been a cornerstone of Sally Rugg's activism. The collective solidarity, emotional backing, mobilization efforts, and commitment to inclusivity have all contributed to her resilience and success. As Rugg continues to navigate the complexities of advocacy, the unwavering support of the LGBTQ community remains a powerful reminder of the strength that comes from unity. Together, they are not just fighting for rights; they are building a legacy of empowerment and change that will resonate for generations to come.

## Coping with personal attacks and threats

In the realm of activism, particularly within the LGBTQ community, the journey is often fraught with challenges that extend beyond the public sphere. For Sally Rugg, personal attacks and threats became a painful reality as she rose to prominence. Coping with these adversities requires not only resilience but also a strategic approach to mental health and community support.

### Understanding the Nature of Attacks

Personal attacks against activists can manifest in various forms: verbal harassment, social media trolling, and even physical threats. According to [?], these attacks are often rooted in deep-seated societal prejudices and a desire to silence voices advocating for change. Sally faced a barrage of online hate, particularly during pivotal moments in her advocacy for marriage equality. This digital hostility is not just noise; it can have profound psychological effects, including anxiety, depression, and a sense of isolation.

### The Psychological Impact

The psychological toll of personal attacks can be significant. Research indicates that repeated exposure to hostile environments can lead to what is known as *vicarious trauma*, where individuals begin to internalize the negativity directed towards them [?]. For Sally, this manifested in moments of self-doubt and fear about her safety. The constant barrage of threats can create a pervasive sense of vulnerability, making it crucial for activists to develop coping strategies.

### Coping Strategies

**Building a Support Network**   One of the most effective ways to cope with personal attacks is to establish a robust support network. Sally found solace in her community—friends, fellow activists, and mental health professionals who understood the unique pressures faced by LGBTQ advocates. According to [?], social support is a critical buffer against the psychological effects of harassment. By surrounding herself with empathetic individuals, Sally was able to process her experiences and gain strength from collective resilience.

**Utilizing Mental Health Resources**   In addition to community support, accessing mental health resources plays a vital role in coping with personal attacks. Therapy can provide a safe space for activists to explore their feelings and develop coping mechanisms. Cognitive Behavioral Therapy (CBT), for instance, has been shown to help individuals reframe negative thoughts and reduce anxiety [?]. Sally engaged in therapy, which allowed her to navigate her emotions and maintain her mental well-being amidst the chaos.

**Engaging in Self-Care** Self-care practices are essential for maintaining mental health, especially for those in high-stress environments like activism. For Sally, this meant prioritizing time for activities that brought her joy and relaxation, such as hiking, reading, and spending time with loved ones. The concept of self-care is not merely indulgent; it is a necessary practice for sustaining long-term activism. According to [?], integrating self-care into one's routine can enhance resilience and prevent burnout.

## Responding to Threats

When confronted with direct threats, it is crucial to have a plan in place. Sally learned to document incidents of harassment, report them to appropriate authorities, and seek legal advice when necessary. This proactive approach not only empowers the individual but also contributes to a larger narrative of accountability. Activists can use their experiences to advocate for policy changes that enhance protections for marginalized communities.

## The Role of Allies

Allies play a pivotal role in the fight against personal attacks on activists. By standing in solidarity, allies can amplify the voices of those being targeted and create a more inclusive environment. Sally's journey highlighted the importance of allyship, as friends and supporters rallied around her during difficult times. This collective action not only offers emotional support but also sends a powerful message that hate will not prevail.

## Conclusion

Coping with personal attacks and threats is an inevitable part of being an activist in today's world. For Sally Rugg, the journey has been one of resilience, community, and self-discovery. By building a support network, utilizing mental health resources, engaging in self-care, and responding strategically to threats, activists can navigate the turbulent waters of advocacy while remaining true to their mission. The fight for LGBTQ rights is not just about policy change; it is also about ensuring the safety and well-being of those who dare to stand up for justice.

## Maintaining resilience and determination

In the face of adversity, the journey of an activist is often punctuated by challenges that test their resolve. For Sally Rugg, maintaining resilience and determination became pivotal not only for her personal growth but also for the broader LGBTQ movement in Australia. Resilience, defined as the ability to recover from setbacks, adapt well to change, and keep going in the face of adversity, is essential for anyone engaged in activism. This section explores the theoretical underpinnings of resilience, the challenges Sally faced, and the strategies she employed to maintain her determination.

### Theoretical Framework of Resilience

Psychological resilience is a concept rooted in positive psychology. According to Masten (2001), resilience is not a trait but a dynamic process that involves the interplay of risk and protective factors. The resilience theory posits that individuals who develop strong coping mechanisms, seek social support, and maintain a positive outlook are more likely to overcome adversities. In Sally's case, her resilience can be attributed to several factors:

- **Social Support:** A strong network of friends, family, and fellow activists provided emotional and practical support during challenging times.

- **Coping Strategies:** Sally employed various coping strategies, such as mindfulness and cognitive restructuring, to manage stress and negative thoughts.

- **Purpose and Meaning:** Her commitment to LGBTQ rights gave her a sense of purpose, motivating her to persist despite challenges.

### Challenges Faced by Sally Rugg

Sally's activism was not without its hurdles. The backlash she faced, including hate speech and personal attacks, was a significant source of stress. For instance, during the peak of the Marriage Equality Campaign, Sally received numerous threats online, which could have deterred a less resilient individual. The psychological toll of such experiences is well-documented; according to the American Psychological Association (2014), exposure to hate speech can lead to increased anxiety, depression, and a sense of isolation among targets.

Moreover, Sally had to navigate the complexities of public scrutiny. As a prominent figure in the LGBTQ community, her actions and statements were often subject to intense analysis. This scrutiny was compounded by societal expectations and the pressure to represent the community positively. The intersectionality of her identity—being a queer woman in a predominantly heteronormative society—added another layer of complexity to her activism.

## Strategies for Maintaining Determination

To maintain her resilience, Sally adopted several strategies:

1. **Building a Support Network:** Sally surrounded herself with like-minded individuals who shared her passion for activism. This network provided a safe space for her to express her feelings and seek advice during tough times.

2. **Engaging in Self-Care:** Recognizing the importance of mental health, Sally prioritized self-care practices. This included regular exercise, meditation, and taking breaks from activism to recharge.

3. **Setting Realistic Goals:** Sally set achievable goals for her activism, breaking down larger objectives into smaller, manageable tasks. This approach not only made her efforts feel more attainable but also provided a sense of accomplishment.

4. **Reflective Practices:** Journaling and reflecting on her experiences allowed Sally to process her emotions and gain perspective. This practice helped her identify patterns in her challenges and celebrate her victories, no matter how small.

5. **Staying Informed and Educated:** By continually educating herself about LGBTQ issues and the history of activism, Sally reinforced her commitment to the cause. Knowledge empowered her to articulate her views effectively and counteract misinformation.

## Examples of Resilience in Action

Sally's resilience was evident during pivotal moments in her activism. For example, after receiving backlash for a public statement advocating for trans rights, she chose to engage with her critics rather than retreat. By participating in community forums and discussions, she not only defended her position but also fostered dialogue about the importance of inclusivity within the LGBTQ movement.

Another instance of her determination was during the final push for marriage equality. Facing intense opposition from conservative groups, Sally organized a series of peaceful protests and educational campaigns. Her ability to mobilize supporters and maintain a positive narrative in the media showcased her commitment to resilience and determination.

## Conclusion

Maintaining resilience and determination is crucial for activists like Sally Rugg who face significant challenges in their pursuit of social justice. By leveraging social support, adopting effective coping strategies, and remaining committed to her purpose, Sally exemplifies how resilience can be cultivated and sustained. Her journey serves as a powerful reminder that while the path of activism is fraught with obstacles, the strength to persevere can lead to meaningful change and inspire others to join the fight for equality.

# Bibliography

[1] Masten, A. S. (2001). Ordinary Magic: Resilience Processes in Development. *American Psychologist*, 56(3), 227-238.

[2] American Psychological Association. (2014). The Impact of Hate Speech on Targeted Groups. Retrieved from [APA Website](https://www.apa.org)

## Overcoming obstacles and achieving success

In the journey of activism, obstacles are not merely roadblocks; they are the crucibles that forge resilience and determination. For Sally Rugg, the path was fraught with challenges, yet each difficulty became a stepping stone toward success. The ability to overcome adversity is often rooted in a combination of personal tenacity, community support, and strategic action.

### Theoretical Framework

To understand the dynamics of overcoming obstacles in activism, we can draw from the *Theory of Resilience*, which posits that individuals can adapt positively despite facing significant adversity. According to Rutter (1987), resilience is not a fixed trait but rather a dynamic process that can be influenced by various factors, including social support, personal beliefs, and coping strategies. This theory can be applied to Sally's experiences as she navigated the tumultuous landscape of LGBTQ advocacy.

### Challenges Faced

Sally's activism was not without its challenges. She faced backlash not only from external sources—such as conservative groups and individuals opposing LGBTQ rights—but also from within her community. The pressure of public scrutiny can lead to a phenomenon known as *imposter syndrome*, where individuals doubt their accomplishments and fear being exposed as a "fraud" (Clance & Imes, 1978). Sally experienced moments of self-doubt, particularly when her efforts were met with hostility.

## Community Support as a Catalyst

One of the most significant factors in overcoming these obstacles was the unwavering support from the LGBTQ community. Community solidarity can serve as a protective buffer against the stressors of activism. For instance, during a particularly challenging campaign for marriage equality, Sally found solace in the camaraderie of fellow activists who shared her vision. This collective strength not only bolstered her resolve but also provided practical support, such as organizing rallies and mobilizing resources.

## Coping Mechanisms

Sally employed several coping mechanisms to navigate the emotional toll of activism. Research indicates that effective coping strategies, such as mindfulness and positive reframing, can enhance resilience (Aldao et al., 2010). Sally often practiced mindfulness techniques, which helped her maintain focus and clarity amidst chaos. By reframing negative experiences as opportunities for growth, she was able to transform setbacks into lessons learned.

## Strategic Action and Adaptability

In the face of adversity, Sally demonstrated remarkable adaptability. The ability to pivot and adjust strategies in response to challenges is a hallmark of successful activists. For example, when faced with legislative hurdles, Sally and her team shifted their approach from direct lobbying to grassroots mobilization, engaging the public through social media campaigns and community outreach. This strategic pivot not only increased visibility for the cause but also galvanized public support, leading to significant legislative victories.

## Examples of Success

Sally's journey is punctuated by numerous successes that emerged from her ability to overcome obstacles. One notable achievement was the successful passage of the Marriage Equality Act in Australia. This victory was not just a personal triumph for Sally but also a monumental moment for the LGBTQ community at large. It exemplified how perseverance in the face of adversity can lead to transformative societal change.

Another example is Sally's role in mentoring young activists, which became a crucial aspect of her legacy. By sharing her experiences and strategies for overcoming challenges, she empowered the next generation to navigate their own paths in activism. This cycle of mentorship not only fosters resilience in others but also strengthens the broader movement.

## Conclusion

In conclusion, the journey of overcoming obstacles and achieving success in activism is multifaceted. It requires a blend of personal resilience, community support, strategic adaptability, and a commitment to the cause. Sally Rugg's story is a testament to the power of perseverance and the impact one individual can have in shaping the narrative of LGBTQ rights. As she continues to inspire others, her legacy serves as a reminder that success is not merely defined by victories but by the courage to rise above challenges and fight for what is right.

# Chapter Three: Impact and Legacy

## Section One: Legislative victories

### Marriage equality in Australia

The journey towards marriage equality in Australia is a tale of resilience, advocacy, and the relentless pursuit of justice. This section delves into the historical context, the sociopolitical landscape, and the key milestones that paved the way for the legalization of same-sex marriage in the country.

### Historical Context

The fight for marriage equality in Australia did not emerge in a vacuum; it was part of a broader struggle for LGBTQ rights that began in the late 20th century. The 1970s marked the first wave of activism, with groups like the Campaign Against Moral Persecution (CAMP) advocating for the decriminalization of homosexuality. However, it wasn't until the 21st century that marriage equality became a focal point.

In 2004, the Australian government amended the Marriage Act to explicitly define marriage as a union between a man and a woman. This legislative move was a significant setback for LGBTQ activists and galvanized the community to intensify their efforts.

### The Rise of Activism

As public sentiment began to shift, particularly in the wake of global movements advocating for marriage equality, Australian activists mobilized to challenge the status quo. Organizations such as Australian Marriage Equality (AME) played a crucial role in raising awareness and lobbying for legislative change. Their campaigns included high-profile events, social media initiatives, and partnerships with influential allies, which helped to bring the issue into the public consciousness.

One notable example was the 2015 "Love is Love" campaign, which featured prominent public figures and celebrities advocating for marriage equality. The campaign successfully humanized the issue, showcasing personal stories of same-sex couples who longed for the same legal recognition as their heterosexual counterparts.

## The 2017 Postal Survey

A pivotal moment in the journey towards marriage equality was the 2017 Australian Marriage Law Postal Survey. The government announced a non-binding postal survey to gauge public opinion on the issue. This decision was met with mixed reactions; while some viewed it as a democratic approach, others criticized it as a delay tactic.

The survey was conducted from September to November 2017 and resulted in a historic turnout, with approximately 79.5% of eligible voters participating. The outcome was overwhelmingly supportive, with 61.6% of respondents in favor of legalizing same-sex marriage. This decisive result reflected a significant shift in public attitudes and provided the momentum needed for legislative change.

## Legislative Change

Following the survey results, the Australian Parliament faced mounting pressure to act. On December 7, 2017, the Marriage Amendment (Definition and Religious Freedoms) Act 2017 was passed, officially legalizing same-sex marriage in Australia. This landmark decision marked a significant victory for LGBTQ activists and allies, culminating years of advocacy and struggle.

The legislation not only allowed same-sex couples to marry but also included provisions aimed at protecting religious freedoms, ensuring that religious institutions could choose whether to perform marriages for same-sex couples. This compromise was crucial in garnering support from various political factions and religious groups, highlighting the complexities involved in the marriage equality debate.

## Impact and Ongoing Challenges

The legalization of marriage equality in Australia had profound implications for LGBTQ individuals and the broader community. It symbolized societal acceptance and recognition of same-sex relationships, fostering a sense of belonging and legitimacy for countless couples. The emotional and psychological benefits of marriage equality cannot be overstated, as it provided a framework for love and commitment that had been denied for so long.

However, the journey did not end with the passage of the Marriage Amendment. LGBTQ activists continue to face challenges, including the need for comprehensive anti-discrimination protections and the recognition of transgender and non-binary identities. The fight for equality is ongoing, as activists work to ensure that the rights achieved are upheld and expanded upon in the years to come.

## Conclusion

In summary, the path to marriage equality in Australia serves as a testament to the power of activism and the importance of public support in enacting social change. It underscores the notion that love, in all its forms, deserves recognition and respect. As we reflect on this journey, we must remain vigilant and committed to advancing the rights of all individuals, ensuring that the legacy of the marriage equality movement continues to inspire future generations of activists.

$$\text{Success} = \text{Advocacy} + \text{Public Support} + \text{Legislative Action} \qquad (14)$$

## Progress in LGBTQ rights

The journey towards equality for LGBTQ individuals has been marked by significant milestones and ongoing struggles. This section explores the progress made in LGBTQ rights, highlighting key legislative changes, societal shifts, and the role of activism in fostering an inclusive environment.

### Legislative Milestones

One of the most pivotal moments in the history of LGBTQ rights in Australia was the legalization of same-sex marriage in 2017. The passage of the Marriage Amendment (Definition and Religious Freedoms) Act 2017 marked a significant victory for LGBTQ activists, culminating years of advocacy and public support. The campaign for marriage equality was not merely about the right to marry; it symbolized a broader fight for recognition, dignity, and equality under the law.

The success of this campaign can be attributed to a combination of factors, including:

+ **Public Support:** Polls indicated a growing acceptance of same-sex relationships among the Australian public. By the time of the postal survey in 2017, approximately 62% of Australians supported marriage equality, reflecting a significant shift in societal attitudes.

+ **Coalition Building:** LGBTQ organizations collaborated with various stakeholders, including religious groups, businesses, and political parties, to build a united front advocating for change. This coalition was instrumental in amplifying the message and reaching a broader audience.

+ **Media Engagement:** The media played a crucial role in shaping public perception. Positive representation of LGBTQ individuals in mainstream media helped humanize the struggle for equality, making it harder for opponents to justify discrimination.

## Anti-Discrimination Laws

In addition to marriage equality, progress has also been made in enacting comprehensive anti-discrimination laws. The Sex Discrimination Act 1984 was amended in 2013 to include protections against discrimination based on sexual orientation and gender identity. This legislative change provided a legal framework for individuals to challenge discriminatory practices in various sectors, including employment, housing, and education.

$$D_{\text{LGBTQ}} = \frac{N_{\text{discrimination}}}{N_{\text{total}}} \times 100 \tag{15}$$

Where: - $D_{\text{LGBTQ}}$ = Discrimination rate against LGBTQ individuals - $N_{\text{discrimination}}$ = Number of reported discrimination cases against LGBTQ individuals - $N_{\text{total}}$ = Total number of discrimination cases reported

This equation illustrates the need for ongoing monitoring of discrimination rates to assess the effectiveness of anti-discrimination laws.

## Cisgender and Transgender Rights

While significant strides have been made for cisgender LGBTQ individuals, the fight for transgender rights remains a pressing issue. Transgender individuals often face unique challenges, including barriers to healthcare, legal recognition, and social acceptance. The introduction of the Australian Government's National Trans and Gender Diverse Health Plan in 2020 aimed to address these issues by providing guidelines for improving healthcare access and outcomes for transgender individuals.

However, the implementation of such policies is often met with resistance. For example, debates surrounding the inclusion of transgender women in women's sports have sparked controversy and highlighted the need for nuanced discussions around gender identity and equality.

## Global Influence and Responsibility

Australia's progress in LGBTQ rights has not only impacted its citizens but has also influenced global conversations about equality. The country's legislative victories serve as a beacon of hope for LGBTQ activists in regions where rights are still severely limited. However, with this influence comes a responsibility to support international LGBTQ rights movements, particularly in countries where individuals face persecution based on their sexual orientation or gender identity.

- **International Advocacy:** Australian activists and organizations have increasingly engaged in international advocacy, partnering with global LGBTQ rights groups to amplify the voices of marginalized communities.

- **Refugee Support:** The establishment of programs to support LGBTQ refugees fleeing persecution has been a crucial step in acknowledging the global nature of the struggle for equality.

## Sustaining Momentum for Future Progress

Despite the progress made, the LGBTQ rights movement must remain vigilant. Ongoing challenges, such as the rise of anti-LGBTQ rhetoric and legislation in various parts of the world, necessitate a sustained commitment to advocacy. The movement must focus on:

- **Intersectionality:** Recognizing the diverse experiences within the LGBTQ community, including those based on race, class, and disability, is essential for creating an inclusive movement.

- **Youth Engagement:** Empowering the next generation of activists through education and mentorship programs ensures the continuation of the fight for equality.

- **Mental Health Initiatives:** Addressing the mental health challenges faced by LGBTQ individuals, particularly youth, is crucial for fostering resilience and well-being.

In conclusion, the progress in LGBTQ rights in Australia reflects a combination of legislative victories, societal acceptance, and the tireless efforts of activists. While significant strides have been made, the journey towards full equality continues. It is imperative to maintain momentum, advocate for the most marginalized, and ensure that the rights achieved are not only protected but expanded upon in the years to come.

## Cisgender and transgender rights

The struggle for cisgender and transgender rights is an integral part of the broader LGBTQ rights movement. While the fight for marriage equality marked a significant milestone, it also highlighted the ongoing challenges faced by transgender individuals and those who do not conform to traditional gender norms. This section explores the theoretical underpinnings, social issues, and notable examples that illustrate the complexities surrounding cisgender and transgender rights.

### Theoretical Framework

Understanding cisgender and transgender rights requires a grasp of gender theory, which posits that gender is a social construct influenced by cultural, historical, and political contexts. Judith Butler, a prominent gender theorist, argues that gender is performative; it is not an inherent quality but rather something that individuals enact through their behaviors and expressions [?]. This perspective challenges the binary understanding of gender and opens the door for recognizing the diverse experiences of transgender individuals.

Transgender rights advocacy is often grounded in the principles of intersectionality, a term coined by Kimberlé Crenshaw. Intersectionality emphasizes the interconnectedness of social categorizations such as race, class, and gender, which can create overlapping systems of discrimination and disadvantage [?]. For transgender individuals, their experiences are shaped not only by their gender identity but also by other social identities they hold, making it crucial to consider these intersections in advocacy efforts.

### Challenges Faced by Transgender Individuals

Despite progress in some areas, transgender individuals face significant challenges that hinder their rights and well-being. Discrimination in various aspects of life, including employment, healthcare, and education, remains pervasive. According to a report by the Human Rights Campaign, nearly 50% of transgender individuals experience unemployment at some point in their lives, often due to bias and discrimination based on their gender identity [?].

Additionally, access to healthcare is a critical issue for transgender individuals. Many face barriers in obtaining gender-affirming care, including hormone therapy and surgeries. The World Professional Association for Transgender Health (WPATH) emphasizes the importance of providing comprehensive healthcare that respects an individual's gender identity [?]. However, many healthcare providers lack the necessary training, leading to inadequate care and increased mental health issues among transgender individuals.

## Legal Protections and Advocacy Efforts

In recent years, there have been notable advancements in legal protections for transgender individuals. For instance, the introduction of anti-discrimination laws in various jurisdictions has provided a legal framework to protect transgender individuals from discrimination in employment, housing, and public accommodations. In Australia, the Sex Discrimination Act was amended in 2013 to include protections for transgender individuals, marking a significant step forward [?].

Advocacy organizations such as the Australian Transgender Support Association (ATSA) and the Human Rights Campaign have played a crucial role in pushing for these legal changes. They have organized campaigns, raised awareness, and provided resources to support transgender individuals navigating legal systems. For example, the "Transgender Day of Remembrance" serves as an annual observance to honor the lives lost to anti-transgender violence, raising awareness about the ongoing struggles faced by the community.

## Notable Examples of Progress

Several landmark cases and initiatives have contributed to the advancement of transgender rights. One notable example is the case of Norrie McDonald, who, in 2014, became the first person in Australia to be recognized as non-binary on legal documents. The New South Wales Births, Deaths, and Marriages Registry allowed Norrie to have their gender recorded as "non-specific," setting a precedent for recognizing non-binary identities in legal frameworks [?].

Moreover, the increasing visibility of transgender individuals in media and politics has played a pivotal role in shaping public perception and acceptance. Figures such as Hannah Gadsby and Georgie Stone have used their platforms to advocate for transgender rights, challenging stereotypes and promoting inclusivity

[?].    Their stories resonate with many, highlighting the importance of representation in fostering understanding and empathy.

## Conclusion

The fight for cisgender and transgender rights remains a critical component of the LGBTQ rights movement. While progress has been made, significant challenges persist.    Advocacy efforts must continue to focus on dismantling systemic discrimination, ensuring access to healthcare, and promoting legal protections for transgender individuals. As society evolves, it is essential to recognize and celebrate the diversity of gender identities, fostering a culture of acceptance and inclusion for all.

## Influencing policy change globally

The impact of Sally Rugg's advocacy extends far beyond the borders of Australia, influencing LGBTQ policy change on a global scale. This phenomenon can be understood through several theoretical frameworks, including social movement theory, which posits that collective action can lead to significant social and political changes. The theory suggests that movements arise in response to perceived injustices and that activists mobilize to challenge the status quo, often resulting in policy reforms.

### Theoretical Framework: Social Movement Theory

Social movement theory provides a lens through which to examine how Rugg's work has inspired similar movements worldwide. According to Charles Tilly, social movements are characterized by sustained campaigns of claim-making that employ a variety of tactics, including protests, lobbying, and media engagement. Rugg's strategic use of these tactics has not only advanced LGBTQ rights in Australia but has also served as a blueprint for activists in other countries facing similar challenges.

### Global Challenges and Discrimination

Despite progress in many nations, LGBTQ individuals continue to face significant discrimination and violence globally. For instance, in regions where anti-LGBTQ laws are still enforced, such as parts of Africa and Eastern Europe, activists encounter severe backlash when advocating for rights. The Global Acceptance Index, which measures the acceptance of LGBTQ individuals in various countries, highlights stark contrasts in societal attitudes and legal protections. Rugg's advocacy has spotlighted these disparities, pushing for international attention and solidarity.

## Case Study: Marriage Equality Beyond Australia

One of the most significant examples of Rugg's influence can be seen in the global movement for marriage equality. Following the successful campaign in Australia, countries such as Taiwan and Costa Rica have made strides toward legalizing same-sex marriage. In Taiwan, the Constitutional Court's 2017 ruling mandating marriage equality was inspired by international movements, including those led by Rugg and her peers. This case illustrates how successful advocacy can create a ripple effect, encouraging other nations to reconsider their laws and policies.

## Transnational Advocacy Networks

Rugg's work has also contributed to the formation of transnational advocacy networks, which play a crucial role in influencing global policy. These networks consist of various stakeholders, including NGOs, activists, and international organizations, working collaboratively to promote LGBTQ rights. By participating in global forums such as the United Nations Human Rights Council, Rugg has helped to elevate the discourse around LGBTQ issues, advocating for universal human rights standards that include protections for sexual and gender minorities.

## Impact of Social Media and Digital Activism

In the digital age, social media has emerged as a powerful tool for advocacy. Rugg's savvy use of platforms like Twitter, Instagram, and Facebook has allowed her to reach a global audience, mobilizing support and raising awareness about LGBTQ issues. For example, the #LoveIsLove campaign, which gained traction during the marriage equality debates, demonstrated how online movements can influence public opinion and, ultimately, policy decisions. Digital activism enables activists to share stories, strategies, and successes, creating a sense of global solidarity among LGBTQ communities.

## Challenges to Global Influence

While Rugg's influence is significant, it is essential to acknowledge the challenges faced by LGBTQ activists worldwide. In many countries, backlash against LGBTQ rights is on the rise, fueled by conservative political movements and religious opposition. For instance, in Hungary and Poland, governments have enacted laws that restrict LGBTQ rights, often citing traditional values as justification. Rugg's work highlights the importance of intersectionality in activism, recognizing that LGBTQ rights are often intertwined with broader human rights issues, including race, gender, and economic justice.

## Conclusion: A Global Legacy

Sally Rugg's efforts to influence policy change globally underscore the interconnectedness of the LGBTQ rights movement. By leveraging social movement theory, engaging in transnational advocacy, and utilizing digital platforms, Rugg has not only advanced LGBTQ rights in Australia but has also inspired a worldwide movement for equality. Her legacy is a testament to the power of collective action and the ongoing struggle for justice, reminding us that while progress has been made, the fight for LGBTQ rights is far from over. The global landscape remains fraught with challenges, but Rugg's influence serves as a beacon of hope and inspiration for activists everywhere.

$$\text{Global Influence} = f(\text{Local Activism, Transnational Networks, Digital Engagement}) \tag{16}$$

## Sustaining momentum for future progress

As we reflect on the achievements of the LGBTQ rights movement, it becomes increasingly clear that sustaining momentum for future progress is paramount. This section delves into the theoretical frameworks that underpin ongoing activism, identifies the challenges faced in maintaining this momentum, and provides examples of successful strategies employed by activists to ensure that the fight for equality and justice continues unabated.

## Theoretical Frameworks

The concept of *social movement theory* offers valuable insights into how movements can sustain momentum over time. Theories such as *resource mobilization theory* emphasize the importance of resources—financial, human, and social—in maintaining activism. According to McCarthy and Zald (1977), successful movements must effectively mobilize resources to maintain organizational structures and foster collective action.

Another relevant framework is *political opportunity structure*, which posits that the external political environment significantly influences a movement's capacity to mobilize and sustain momentum. Tilly (1978) suggests that favorable political conditions, such as supportive legislation and public opinion, can enhance a movement's effectiveness. For instance, the legalization of same-sex marriage in Australia in 2017 created a more favorable landscape for LGBTQ activism, enabling organizations to build on this success and tackle other pressing issues, such as transgender rights and discrimination.

## Challenges to Sustaining Momentum

Despite these frameworks, several challenges threaten the sustainability of momentum within the LGBTQ rights movement. One significant issue is *complacency*. Following landmark victories, such as marriage equality, there can be a tendency among activists and allies to relax their efforts, mistakenly believing that the fight for LGBTQ rights is complete. This complacency can lead to a loss of visibility and support for ongoing issues, such as homelessness among LGBTQ youth, healthcare access, and violence against transgender individuals.

Another challenge is *fragmentation* within the movement. As the LGBTQ community becomes increasingly diverse, with distinct needs and priorities emerging among various subgroups (e.g., transgender individuals, LGBTQ people of color), there is a risk of fragmentation. This can dilute the movement's overall effectiveness and hinder collective action. The intersectionality framework, introduced by Crenshaw (1989), highlights the necessity of addressing these diverse identities and experiences to create a unified front.

## Successful Strategies for Sustaining Momentum

To counter these challenges, activists have adopted several successful strategies that can be employed to sustain momentum for future progress.

**1. Continuous Education and Advocacy**  Ongoing education and advocacy are crucial for maintaining awareness of LGBTQ issues. Organizations like *The Equality Campaign* have developed comprehensive educational programs aimed at schools, workplaces, and community centers. These initiatives not only raise awareness but also foster allyship, ensuring that the broader community remains engaged in the fight for equality.

**2. Building Alliances**   Forming alliances with other social justice movements can amplify the impact of LGBTQ activism. Collaborations with movements focused on racial justice, women's rights, and disability rights can create a broader coalition advocating for systemic change. For example, the *Black Lives Matter* movement has highlighted the experiences of Black LGBTQ individuals, emphasizing the need for intersectional approaches to activism.

**3. Leveraging Technology and Social Media**   In the digital age, technology plays a pivotal role in sustaining momentum. Social media platforms provide a space for activists to share stories, mobilize supporters, and raise funds. Campaigns such as *#TransRightsAreHumanRights* utilize hashtags to create viral movements, drawing attention to pressing issues facing the transgender community and ensuring that these topics remain at the forefront of public discourse.

**4. Engaging Youth Activists**   Empowering the next generation of activists is essential for sustaining momentum. Programs that mentor young LGBTQ individuals and encourage their participation in activism can invigorate the movement. Initiatives like *The Trevor Project's* youth leadership programs equip young people with the tools necessary to advocate for their rights and the rights of their peers.

## Conclusion

In conclusion, sustaining momentum for future progress in the LGBTQ rights movement requires a multifaceted approach that combines theoretical insights with practical strategies.   By recognizing the challenges of complacency and fragmentation, activists can implement effective measures to ensure that the fight for equality continues. Through continuous education, strategic alliances, the use of technology, and the engagement of youth, the LGBTQ movement can build upon its past successes and strive for a more inclusive and equitable future. As we move forward, it is imperative that we remain vigilant and committed to the ongoing struggle for justice and equality, ensuring that the legacy of activists like Sally Rugg lives on in the hearts and minds of future generations.

# Section Two: LGBTQ youth empowerment

## Mentoring programs and support initiatives

Mentoring programs and support initiatives play a crucial role in empowering LGBTQ youth, providing them with the guidance, resources, and community support necessary to navigate the complexities of their identities and societal challenges. These programs are designed to foster resilience, build confidence, and promote personal growth among young individuals who often face unique obstacles related to their sexual orientation or gender identity.

## Theoretical Framework

The effectiveness of mentoring programs can be understood through several psychological and sociological theories. One pertinent theory is Bandura's Social Learning Theory, which posits that individuals learn behaviors and develop skills through observation, imitation, and modeling. In the context of LGBTQ mentoring, youth can observe positive role models who have navigated similar challenges, thereby fostering a sense of hope and possibility for their own futures.

Additionally, the concept of *intersectionality*, coined by Kimberlé Crenshaw, emphasizes the importance of recognizing how various forms of identity (such as race, class, and gender) intersect and impact individuals' experiences. Mentoring programs that incorporate an intersectional approach can address the diverse needs of LGBTQ youth, ensuring that all participants feel seen, valued, and supported.

## Challenges Faced by LGBTQ Youth

LGBTQ youth often encounter a myriad of challenges, including:

+ **Social Isolation:** Many young people in the LGBTQ community experience feelings of isolation due to rejection from family, peers, and society at large. This isolation can lead to mental health issues such as depression and anxiety.

+ **Discrimination and Bullying:** LGBTQ youth frequently face bullying and discrimination in schools and social settings, which can hinder their academic performance and overall well-being.

+ **Lack of Resources:** Many LGBTQ youth lack access to resources that can support their personal development, such as counseling services, educational materials, and safe spaces.

- **Identity Exploration:** The journey of self-discovery can be particularly challenging for LGBTQ youth, who may struggle with acceptance and understanding of their identities.

## Examples of Successful Mentoring Programs

1. **The Trevor Project:** This organization offers a variety of support services for LGBTQ youth, including a 24/7 crisis hotline and online resources. Their mentorship programs connect young individuals with trained mentors who provide guidance and support, helping them navigate challenges related to their identities.

2. **Big Brothers Big Sisters of America:** This national mentoring organization has implemented programs specifically for LGBTQ youth. By pairing them with supportive adult mentors, they help foster resilience and promote positive life choices.

3. **OUT for Sustainability:** This initiative focuses on creating mentoring opportunities within the LGBTQ community that emphasize environmental sustainability. By connecting LGBTQ youth with mentors in sustainability fields, they empower young individuals to pursue careers that align with their passions and values.

## Impact of Mentoring Programs

The impact of mentoring programs on LGBTQ youth is profound. Research indicates that participants in mentoring programs experience:

- **Increased Self-Esteem:** Mentoring relationships can significantly enhance self-esteem and self-worth among LGBTQ youth, providing them with the affirmation they often lack in other areas of their lives.

- **Improved Academic Performance:** Mentored youth tend to perform better academically, as they receive guidance and support in navigating educational challenges.

- **Enhanced Coping Skills:** Through mentorship, youth learn effective coping strategies for dealing with discrimination and social pressures, equipping them with tools to manage stress and adversity.

- **Stronger Community Connections:** Mentoring fosters a sense of belonging and community among LGBTQ youth, helping them build supportive networks that can last a lifetime.

## Conclusion

In conclusion, mentoring programs and support initiatives serve as vital lifelines for LGBTQ youth, offering them the resources and guidance they need to thrive. By fostering resilience, promoting self-acceptance, and providing positive role models, these programs not only empower young individuals but also contribute to the broader movement for LGBTQ rights and acceptance. As Sally Rugg's advocacy demonstrates, investing in the next generation of LGBTQ leaders is essential for sustaining progress and ensuring a brighter future for all.

# Education and awareness campaigns

Education and awareness campaigns have played a pivotal role in advancing LGBTQ rights and promoting understanding within society. These initiatives aim to inform the public about LGBTQ issues, dispel myths, and foster a culture of acceptance and inclusivity. Sally Rugg has been at the forefront of such campaigns, recognizing the profound impact that education can have on reducing stigma and discrimination.

## Theoretical Framework

The theoretical underpinnings of education and awareness campaigns can be examined through the lens of social learning theory, proposed by Albert Bandura. This theory posits that people learn from one another through observation, imitation, and modeling. In the context of LGBTQ education, individuals can learn about diverse sexual orientations and gender identities, leading to greater empathy and understanding. The equation representing the social learning process can be expressed as:

$$B = f(E, O, P)$$

Where: - $B$ = Behavior - $E$ = Environment - $O$ = Observational learning - $P$ = Personal factors

This equation illustrates that behavior (such as acceptance of LGBTQ individuals) is a function of environmental influences, observational learning, and personal experiences. By providing educational resources and opportunities for interaction, campaigns can shift societal norms and encourage positive behaviors toward the LGBTQ community.

## Key Problems Addressed

Despite progress, significant challenges remain in the realm of LGBTQ education. One major issue is the prevalence of misinformation and stereotypes that perpetuate discrimination. For instance, many individuals still hold misconceptions about the causes of homosexuality, believing it to be a choice or a mental disorder. Education campaigns aim to correct these misunderstandings by providing factual information, such as the consensus among major health organizations that being LGBTQ is a natural variation of human sexuality.

Another challenge is the lack of representation in educational curricula. Many schools do not include LGBTQ topics in their sex education programs, leading to a gap in knowledge for both LGBTQ youth and their peers. This lack of representation can contribute to feelings of isolation among LGBTQ students, who may feel their identities are not acknowledged or validated within the educational system.

## Successful Examples

Sally Rugg's involvement in various education and awareness campaigns has yielded significant outcomes. One notable initiative is the "Safe Schools" program, which aims to create safe and inclusive environments for LGBTQ students in Australian schools. The program provides resources and training for educators to address bullying and discrimination, fostering a supportive atmosphere for all students. Research has shown that schools implementing such programs report a decrease in bullying incidents and an increase in students' feelings of safety and belonging.

Another effective campaign is the "Wear It Purple" day, which encourages young people to wear purple to show support for LGBTQ youth. This initiative not only raises awareness but also provides a visible symbol of solidarity, reminding LGBTQ youth that they are not alone. The campaign has gained traction across schools, universities, and workplaces, generating conversations about acceptance and diversity.

## Impact on LGBTQ Youth

Education and awareness campaigns have a profound impact on LGBTQ youth. By increasing visibility and representation, these initiatives help young people feel seen and validated. For example, programs that include LGBTQ history and contributions in school curricula can instill pride in students' identities and foster a sense of belonging. Furthermore, mentorship programs that connect LGBTQ youth with role models can provide guidance and support, helping them navigate the complexities of their identities in a heteronormative society.

The importance of mental health support cannot be overstated. Education campaigns often incorporate mental health resources, emphasizing the significance of seeking help and promoting well-being among LGBTQ youth. Studies indicate that access to supportive resources can significantly reduce rates of depression and anxiety in LGBTQ individuals, contributing to healthier and more resilient communities.

## Conclusion

In conclusion, education and awareness campaigns are essential components of the broader LGBTQ rights movement. By addressing misconceptions, providing representation, and fostering inclusivity, these initiatives empower LGBTQ individuals and promote societal change. Sally Rugg's dedication to these efforts exemplifies the transformative power of education in creating a more just and equitable world for all. As we look to the future, continued investment in education and awareness will be crucial in sustaining progress and ensuring that LGBTQ voices are heard and valued.

## Speaking engagements at schools and universities

Sally Rugg's speaking engagements at schools and universities have become a vital aspect of her activism, providing a platform to educate and empower the next generation. These engagements are not merely speeches; they are interactive dialogues that challenge students to think critically about LGBTQ issues, fostering an environment of inclusivity and understanding.

### The Importance of Education in Activism

Education plays a pivotal role in dismantling stereotypes and prejudices. According to [?], education should be a practice of freedom, where individuals learn to question and transform their world. Rugg embodies this philosophy by engaging with students, encouraging them to reflect on their own beliefs and biases regarding LGBTQ identities.

The theory of *Critical Pedagogy* posits that education should not just transmit knowledge but also empower students to challenge the status quo [?]. Rugg's approach aligns with this by promoting critical thinking, urging students to analyze the societal constructs surrounding gender and sexuality.

## Addressing Common Problems in LGBTQ Education

Despite the progress made in LGBTQ rights, many schools still lack comprehensive education on these topics. A survey conducted by the *Australian Human Rights Commission* found that 60% of LGBTQ students felt unsafe at school due to their sexual orientation [?]. Rugg addresses this alarming statistic head-on during her engagements.

One common problem is the prevalence of *bullying and harassment* in educational settings. Rugg shares personal anecdotes about her own experiences with bullying, creating a relatable narrative that resonates with students. She emphasizes the importance of allyship, stating:

> "Being an ally is not just about standing with us; it's about using your voice to speak out against injustice."

This approach not only humanizes the statistics but also empowers students to take action within their own communities.

## Examples of Engagements

Rugg has spoken at numerous institutions, from high schools to universities, tailoring her message to suit the audience. For instance, during a visit to *Melbourne High School*, she led a workshop titled *"Understanding Gender Diversity"*, which included interactive activities that allowed students to explore their own identities and the spectrum of gender.

At *University of Sydney*, she delivered a keynote address during Pride Week, where she discussed the historical context of LGBTQ rights in Australia. She highlighted significant milestones, such as the legalization of same-sex marriage, and encouraged students to reflect on how they can contribute to ongoing advocacy efforts. Her speeches often include a call to action, urging students to participate in local LGBTQ initiatives and support organizations like *Minus18* and *The Equality Campaign*.

## Impact of Engagements

The impact of Rugg's engagements extends beyond the immediate audience. Feedback from students often highlights a newfound understanding and empathy towards LGBTQ issues. Many report feeling inspired to become advocates themselves.

For example, after a presentation at *La Trobe University*, a group of students organized a *"Day of Silence"* to raise awareness about the bullying faced by LGBTQ peers. This grassroots initiative exemplifies how Rugg's influence can catalyze action and foster a culture of support within educational institutions.

Moreover, Rugg's engagements contribute to a broader cultural shift. By addressing LGBTQ issues in academic settings, she helps to normalize conversations around gender and sexuality, paving the way for future generations to embrace diversity without fear or prejudice.

## Conclusion

Sally Rugg's speaking engagements at schools and universities are more than just lectures; they are transformative experiences that educate, empower, and inspire young minds. By integrating critical pedagogy and personal narratives, Rugg successfully addresses the challenges faced by LGBTQ individuals, fostering a sense of community and encouraging students to become allies in the fight for equality.

Through her efforts, Rugg not only shapes the narrative of LGBTQ rights in Australia but also cultivates a new generation of activists ready to carry the torch forward.

## Amplifying young voices and stories

The importance of amplifying young voices in the LGBTQ community cannot be overstated. As society evolves, the narratives of the youth become pivotal in shaping the future of activism and advocacy. Young LGBTQ individuals often face unique challenges that differ from those encountered by older generations, including issues related to identity, acceptance, and mental health. This section explores the strategies employed by Sally Rugg and other activists to elevate these voices, the theoretical frameworks that support this initiative, and the impact of such efforts on the community at large.

### Theoretical Framework

The amplification of young voices is grounded in several key theories of social change and empowerment. One such theory is **Youth Participatory Action Research (YPAR)**, which emphasizes the involvement of young people in the research process to address issues that affect them directly. According to [?], YPAR not only empowers youth but also encourages critical consciousness, enabling them to analyze their social conditions and advocate for change.

Another relevant theory is **Intersectionality,** as articulated by [5]. Intersectionality posits that individuals experience overlapping forms of discrimination based on various social identities, including gender, race, and sexual orientation. By recognizing the diverse experiences within the LGBTQ youth community, activists can tailor their approaches to advocacy, ensuring that all voices are heard and valued.

## Challenges Faced by LGBTQ Youth

Despite the progress made in LGBTQ rights, young individuals still confront significant challenges, including:

+ **Mental Health Issues:** Studies indicate that LGBTQ youth are at a higher risk for mental health issues, including depression and anxiety, often stemming from societal stigma and discrimination [?].

+ **Bullying and Harassment:** Many LGBTQ youth face bullying in schools, leading to a hostile environment that stifles their ability to express themselves freely [?].

+ **Lack of Representation:** Young LGBTQ individuals often feel marginalized in media and political discourse, which can lead to feelings of isolation and invisibility [?].

## Strategies for Amplification

Sally Rugg has implemented various strategies to amplify young voices, including:

1. **Mentorship Programs:** These programs pair experienced activists with LGBTQ youth, providing guidance, support, and a platform for young voices to be heard. For instance, Rugg's mentorship initiatives have facilitated workshops where youth can share their stories and learn advocacy skills.

2. **Social Media Campaigns:** Leveraging platforms such as Instagram and TikTok, Rugg has encouraged young activists to share their stories through hashtags like #MyPrideStory. This not only raises awareness but also fosters a sense of community among youth.

3. **Speaking Engagements:** By organizing events at schools and universities, Rugg has created spaces for young activists to share their experiences. These

engagements often include panel discussions where youth can voice their concerns and aspirations, thus shaping the narrative around LGBTQ issues.

4. **Storytelling Initiatives:** Programs that focus on storytelling allow LGBTQ youth to express their identities and experiences creatively. Rugg has been instrumental in supporting initiatives like "StoryCorps," which records personal narratives and shares them widely, ensuring that young voices resonate beyond their immediate communities.

## Impact on the Community

The amplification of young voices has led to several positive outcomes for the LGBTQ community:

+ **Increased Visibility:** By sharing their stories, young LGBTQ individuals contribute to greater visibility and representation, challenging stereotypes and fostering understanding among the broader population.

+ **Policy Influence:** Engaged and empowered youth have begun to influence policy discussions, advocating for changes that reflect their needs and experiences. For example, youth-led campaigns have successfully lobbied for inclusive curricula in schools that address LGBTQ issues.

+ **Community Building:** Amplifying young voices fosters a sense of belonging and community, as youth connect with others who share similar experiences. This sense of community is crucial for mental health and resilience, providing support networks that combat isolation.

## Conclusion

In conclusion, the work of Sally Rugg in amplifying young LGBTQ voices is not just about raising awareness; it is a transformative approach to activism that empowers the next generation. By employing theoretical frameworks such as YPAR and intersectionality, Rugg has created a robust platform for youth to express their stories and advocate for their rights. The challenges faced by LGBTQ youth are significant, but through mentorship, social media engagement, and storytelling initiatives, their voices are being heard louder than ever. As Rugg continues her work, the legacy of these young activists will undoubtedly shape the future of LGBTQ rights and advocacy.

## Creating a brighter future for LGBTQ youth

In recent years, the conversation surrounding LGBTQ youth has evolved, highlighting the urgent need for supportive environments that foster acceptance, understanding, and empowerment. Sally Rugg's advocacy work has been pivotal in addressing the challenges faced by LGBTQ youth, focusing on creating a brighter future through mentorship, education, and community engagement.

## The Importance of Mentoring Programs

Mentoring programs have emerged as a crucial component in supporting LGBTQ youth. These initiatives provide young individuals with role models who understand their unique experiences and challenges. Research suggests that mentorship can significantly impact the mental health and well-being of LGBTQ youth, reducing feelings of isolation and increasing resilience. According to the *Youth Mentoring Research Update* (2018), youth who participate in mentoring programs are 55% more likely to enroll in college and 78% more likely to volunteer regularly in their communities.

## Education and Awareness Campaigns

Education is a powerful tool for dismantling prejudice and fostering inclusivity. Sally Rugg has championed various education and awareness campaigns aimed at schools and communities. These initiatives focus on teaching the importance of diversity, acceptance, and the history of LGBTQ rights. For instance, the *Safe Schools Coalition* in Australia has been instrumental in providing training for educators to create inclusive classrooms. According to a study conducted by the *Australian Institute of Health and Welfare* (2020), schools that implement LGBTQ-inclusive curricula report a 30% decrease in bullying incidents.

## Speaking Engagements at Schools and Universities

Sally Rugg's speaking engagements at schools and universities serve as a platform for sharing personal stories and educating young people about LGBTQ issues. These events not only empower LGBTQ youth but also encourage allies to take an active role in promoting inclusivity. By sharing her journey, Rugg inspires students to embrace their identities and advocate for their rights. In a survey conducted by the *National Union of Students* (NUS) in 2021, 85% of students reported that attending such talks made them more supportive of their LGBTQ peers.

## Amplifying Young Voices and Stories

Amplifying the voices of LGBTQ youth is essential for fostering a sense of belonging and validating their experiences. Rugg has been instrumental in creating platforms where young people can share their stories, whether through social media campaigns or community events. The *It Gets Better Project*, which started as a viral video campaign, has evolved into a global movement that empowers LGBTQ youth by sharing uplifting stories of resilience. According to their 2022 report, over 50,000 videos have been submitted, reaching millions of viewers and providing hope to countless young individuals.

## Creating Safe Spaces

Creating safe spaces for LGBTQ youth is fundamental in promoting mental health and well-being. These spaces, whether physical or virtual, allow young people to express themselves without fear of judgment or discrimination. Organizations like *Headspace* have developed programs specifically designed for LGBTQ youth, offering counseling and support services. A study by *The Trevor Project* (2021) found that LGBTQ youth who have access to affirming spaces report lower rates of depression and suicidal ideation compared to those who do not.

## The Role of Intersectionality in Advocacy

In advocating for a brighter future for LGBTQ youth, it is crucial to recognize the intersectionality of identities. Sally Rugg emphasizes the importance of understanding how race, gender, and socioeconomic status intersect with sexual orientation and gender identity. By addressing these complexities, advocacy efforts can be more inclusive and effective. For example, the *Black LGBTQIA+ Migrant Project* focuses on the unique challenges faced by LGBTQ individuals of color, ensuring that their voices are heard within the broader LGBTQ movement.

## Conclusion

Creating a brighter future for LGBTQ youth requires a multifaceted approach that includes mentorship, education, safe spaces, and intersectional advocacy. Sally Rugg's tireless efforts in these areas have laid the groundwork for a more inclusive society where LGBTQ youth can thrive. By empowering young people and amplifying their voices, we can foster a generation that embraces diversity and champions equality, ensuring that the future is indeed brighter for all.

# Section Three: Personal growth and reflection

## Evolution of Sally Rugg as an activist

Sally Rugg's journey as an activist is a compelling narrative of growth, resilience, and transformation. Her evolution can be understood through various lenses, including personal experiences, social movements, and theoretical frameworks that underpin activism. This section explores the key milestones in Rugg's development as a leading figure in the LGBTQ rights movement, highlighting her responses to challenges, her strategic choices, and the broader implications of her work.

### From Personal Struggles to Public Advocacy

Rugg's activism did not emerge in a vacuum; it was deeply rooted in her personal experiences as a queer individual navigating a heteronormative society. The early struggles she faced—bullying, discrimination, and familial rejection—shaped her understanding of the systemic inequalities that marginalized LGBTQ individuals. According to *Critical Theory*, particularly the works of Theodor Adorno and Max Horkheimer, the personal is political. Rugg's early life experiences exemplify this notion, illustrating how personal struggles can catalyze political engagement.

As Rugg transitioned from a personal narrative to a public platform, she began to articulate her experiences in ways that resonated with others. She utilized storytelling as a powerful tool for advocacy, engaging audiences emotionally and intellectually. This aligns with *Narrative Theory*, which posits that stories can foster empathy and understanding, ultimately mobilizing individuals toward collective action.

### Strategic Engagement with LGBTQ Organizations

Rugg's involvement with LGBTQ organizations marked a significant turning point in her activism. She joined groups that aligned with her values, such as *Australian Marriage Equality* and *GetUp!*, where she honed her skills in grassroots organizing and strategic communication. Rugg's ability to collaborate with diverse coalitions reflects the principles of *Intersectionality*, as articulated by Kimberlé Crenshaw. By recognizing the interconnected nature of social categorizations, Rugg was able to advocate for a broader spectrum of LGBTQ rights, including those of marginalized subgroups within the community.

Her co-founding of the Marriage Equality Campaign exemplifies her strategic acumen. Rugg recognized that marriage equality was not just a legal issue but also a cultural one. By framing the campaign in terms of love and commitment, she effectively shifted public perception, making the issue relatable to a wider audience. This approach mirrors the *Framing Theory* in social movements, which emphasizes the importance of narrative construction in shaping public discourse.

## Resilience in the Face of Adversity

Throughout her activism, Rugg faced significant challenges, including backlash from conservative factions and personal attacks. Her resilience can be analyzed through the lens of *Psychological Resilience Theory*, which suggests that individuals can develop coping strategies to navigate adversity. Rugg's ability to maintain her focus and commitment to her cause, despite facing hate speech and threats, demonstrates her psychological fortitude.

Moreover, Rugg's engagement with the LGBTQ community provided a vital support network. The sense of belonging and solidarity she cultivated among peers not only bolstered her resolve but also reinforced the collective nature of activism. As noted by *Social Identity Theory*, group membership can enhance an individual's self-esteem and motivation, further empowering Rugg to continue her work.

## Impact on Policy and Legislative Change

Rugg's evolution as an activist culminated in her significant contributions to policy and legislative change in Australia. Her advocacy played a crucial role in the passage of marriage equality legislation, a landmark victory for the LGBTQ community. This achievement can be understood through the lens of *Policy Change Theory*, which posits that successful advocacy often hinges on strategic alliances, effective communication, and public mobilization.

Rugg's impactful speeches and public appearances galvanized support for the movement, illustrating the power of rhetoric in social change. Drawing from *Persuasion Theory*, her ability to appeal to both emotional and rational aspects of her audience was instrumental in shifting public opinion. By framing LGBTQ rights as a matter of justice and equality, Rugg effectively positioned the movement within the broader human rights discourse.

## Reflection and Continuous Growth

As Rugg reflects on her journey, it is evident that her evolution as an activist is ongoing. The lessons she has learned—about intersectionality, resilience, and the importance of community—continue to shape her approach to advocacy. The concept of *Lifelong Learning* in activism emphasizes the need for continuous growth and adaptation in response to changing social dynamics.

Rugg's commitment to mentoring the next generation of activists further underscores her understanding of the importance of fostering new leaders within the LGBTQ community. By sharing her experiences and insights, she not only empowers others but also ensures that the movement remains vibrant and responsive to emerging challenges.

In conclusion, Sally Rugg's evolution as an activist is a testament to her personal journey, strategic engagement, resilience, and commitment to social justice. Her story exemplifies the transformative power of activism, illustrating how individual experiences can catalyze broader societal change. As Rugg continues to advocate for LGBTQ rights, her legacy serves as an inspiration for future generations, reminding us all of the importance of standing up for equality and justice.

## Lessons learned and personal development

Sally Rugg's journey through the tumultuous landscape of LGBTQ activism has been marked by profound lessons and personal growth. Each challenge faced has not only shaped her as a leader but also provided critical insights into the nature of activism, resilience, and the importance of community.

### Embracing Vulnerability

One of the most significant lessons Sally learned is the power of vulnerability. In a society that often demands strength and stoicism, she discovered that sharing her struggles and fears could foster deeper connections with others. This realization aligns with Brené Brown's theory of vulnerability, which posits that it is essential for authentic connection and courage. By openly discussing her experiences with bullying, discrimination, and personal attacks, Sally has encouraged others to embrace their own vulnerabilities, creating a ripple effect of support within the LGBTQ community.

$$C = \frac{V}{S} \tag{17}$$

Where $C$ is connection, $V$ is vulnerability, and $S$ is strength. This equation suggests that true connection is maximized when vulnerability is present, even in the face of adversity.

### The Importance of Intersectionality

Sally's activism has also illuminated the critical importance of intersectionality. She learned that the fight for LGBTQ rights cannot be isolated from other social justice movements. The work of Kimberlé Crenshaw highlights how overlapping identities—such as race, gender, and socioeconomic status—affect individuals' experiences of oppression. Sally's commitment to intersectional activism has led her to collaborate with diverse groups, amplifying marginalized voices within the LGBTQ community.

For instance, during her advocacy for marriage equality, she recognized the unique challenges faced by LGBTQ individuals of color and those with disabilities. This awareness prompted her to include intersectional perspectives in her public speeches and campaigns, fostering a more inclusive movement.

## Resilience Through Community Support

Another pivotal lesson for Sally has been the role of community in fostering resilience. Activism can be an isolating experience, often accompanied by backlash and personal attacks. However, Sally learned that leaning on her community for support could provide the strength needed to persevere. This communal resilience is supported by social support theory, which asserts that individuals with strong social networks are better equipped to cope with stress and adversity.

Sally has actively worked to create safe spaces for LGBTQ youth, where they can find solidarity and encouragement. This proactive approach not only empowers young activists but also reinforces the idea that collective strength is crucial in the face of societal challenges.

## Continuous Learning and Adaptation

Sally's journey has also underscored the necessity of continuous learning and adaptation. The landscape of activism is ever-changing, and staying informed about new developments, theories, and strategies is vital. Sally has embraced a growth mindset, which Carol Dweck defines as the belief that abilities and intelligence can be developed through dedication and hard work. This mindset has allowed her to adapt her strategies and approaches in response to the evolving needs of the LGBTQ community.

For example, when faced with the rise of online hate speech and cyberbullying, Sally sought out training in digital advocacy and online safety. This proactive approach not only enhanced her own skills but also equipped her to educate others on how to navigate these challenges effectively.

## Self-Care as a Fundamental Practice

Lastly, Sally has learned the importance of self-care in sustaining her activism. The emotional toll of fighting for justice can lead to burnout if not managed properly. Sally has integrated self-care practices into her routine, recognizing that taking care of herself is essential for her to continue her work. This realization aligns with the principles of self-care theory, which emphasizes the importance of individual well-being in the context of social change.

Sally advocates for self-care within the LGBTQ community, encouraging others to prioritize their mental and emotional health. This holistic approach not only benefits individual activists but also strengthens the movement as a whole.

In conclusion, the lessons learned throughout Sally Rugg's journey reflect a deep commitment to personal development and the evolution of her activism. By embracing vulnerability, understanding intersectionality, fostering community resilience, committing to continuous learning, and prioritizing self-care, she has not only grown as an individual but has also inspired countless others to do the same. Her journey is a testament to the idea that personal growth and activism are intertwined, each feeding into the other to create a more inclusive and just society.

## Intersectionality in activism

Intersectionality is a critical framework that examines how various social identities—such as race, gender, sexuality, and class—intersect to shape individual experiences and systemic oppression. Coined by legal scholar Kimberlé Crenshaw in 1989, intersectionality emphasizes that people do not experience discrimination in isolated categories; rather, their identities overlap, creating unique challenges and privileges. In the context of LGBTQ activism, understanding intersectionality is vital for creating inclusive movements that address the diverse needs of all individuals within the community.

### Theoretical Foundations

Intersectionality posits that traditional approaches to social justice often fail to account for the complexity of people's lives. For instance, a white, cisgender gay man may experience privilege in certain contexts while facing discrimination in others. Conversely, a queer woman of color may confront compounded challenges due to her race, gender, and sexual orientation. This multiplicity of identities necessitates a more nuanced understanding of activism.

Crenshaw's work highlights that the legal system often overlooks the experiences of those at the intersection of multiple marginalized identities. She argues that the law must evolve to recognize these overlapping identities to address the unique forms of discrimination they face. This theoretical foundation is crucial for LGBTQ activists like Sally Rugg, who strive to create a more equitable society.

## Challenges in Intersectional Activism

While intersectionality provides a framework for understanding diverse experiences, it also presents several challenges for activists. One major issue is the tendency for mainstream LGBTQ movements to prioritize the voices and concerns of more privileged members of the community, often sidelining those who are marginalized within the LGBTQ spectrum. This can lead to the erasure of critical issues affecting LGBTQ people of color, transgender individuals, and those from lower socioeconomic backgrounds.

For example, during the fight for marriage equality in Australia, discussions predominantly centered around the rights of cisgender, white gay couples. While this was a significant victory, it overshadowed the pressing needs of transgender individuals seeking legal recognition and protection from discrimination. Activists must remain vigilant to ensure that all voices are heard and that the movement does not become exclusive.

## Examples of Intersectional Activism

Sally Rugg exemplifies intersectional activism through her commitment to inclusivity within the LGBTQ movement. She has consistently advocated for the rights of marginalized groups, recognizing that the fight for equality must encompass all facets of identity. Rugg's work with organizations such as the Marriage Equality Campaign and her involvement in various coalitions highlight her dedication to intersectional principles.

One notable initiative was her participation in the "Queer People of Color" movement, which aimed to amplify the voices of LGBTQ individuals from diverse racial and ethnic backgrounds. By collaborating with activists from different communities, Rugg helped to address issues like police violence, healthcare disparities, and cultural stigmas that disproportionately affect LGBTQ people of color.

Moreover, Rugg's efforts to include transgender rights in broader LGBTQ advocacy demonstrate her understanding of intersectionality. She has spoken out against anti-trans legislation and worked to ensure that transgender voices are central in discussions about rights and recognition. This approach not only strengthens the LGBTQ movement but also fosters solidarity among various marginalized groups.

## The Importance of Intersectionality in Future Activism

As the landscape of activism continues to evolve, the importance of intersectionality cannot be overstated. Future activists must embrace this framework to create movements that are truly inclusive and representative of all identities. By prioritizing intersectionality, activists can address systemic inequalities and work towards a society where everyone, regardless of their identity, can thrive.

In conclusion, intersectionality is a powerful lens through which to view activism. For Sally Rugg and her contemporaries, understanding and applying intersectional principles is essential for building a more inclusive and effective LGBTQ movement. As the fight for equality progresses, embracing the complexity of identities will ensure that no one is left behind, paving the way for a future where diversity is celebrated, and justice is achieved for all.

## Balancing activism and self-care

In the high-stakes world of activism, where the fight for justice can often feel like a relentless uphill battle, the importance of balancing activism with self-care cannot be overstated. For Sally Rugg, this balance is not just a personal necessity; it is a fundamental aspect of sustainable activism. The emotional and physical toll of advocating for LGBTQ rights can lead to burnout, anxiety, and even depression if not managed properly.

## The Theory of Self-Care in Activism

The theory of self-care emphasizes the necessity of maintaining one's physical, emotional, and mental well-being as a foundation for effective activism. According to the *Self-Care Framework* proposed by the World Health Organization, self-care involves a range of activities that individuals engage in to maintain health and well-being. The framework outlines three primary dimensions of self-care: personal, community, and societal.

In the context of activism, personal self-care refers to the individual practices that activists adopt to recharge and rejuvenate themselves. This could include engaging in hobbies, practicing mindfulness, or simply taking time away from the demands of activism. Community self-care emphasizes the importance of support networks among activists, where individuals can share their experiences, provide emotional support, and collaborate on strategies to cope with the pressures of advocacy. Lastly, societal self-care looks at the broader systems that either support or hinder the well-being of activists, such as workplace policies, mental health resources, and societal attitudes towards activism.

## Challenges in Balancing Activism and Self-Care

Sally Rugg, like many activists, faces significant challenges in maintaining this balance. The pervasive culture of urgency in activism often leads individuals to prioritize their cause over their own well-being. This can result in a phenomenon known as *activist burnout*, characterized by emotional exhaustion, reduced efficacy, and a sense of disillusionment.

Consider the following equation that symbolizes the relationship between activism and self-care:

$$\text{Well-being} = \text{Activism Efforts} - \text{Burnout} \tag{18}$$

Where Well-being represents the overall health of the activist, Activism Efforts denotes the time and energy invested in advocacy, and Burnout quantifies the negative impact of neglecting self-care. A negative value in this equation indicates that the activist's well-being is compromised, underscoring the need for a balance.

## Practical Strategies for Self-Care

To combat burnout, Sally has implemented several practical strategies for self-care, which can serve as a model for other activists:

- **Setting Boundaries:** Sally emphasizes the importance of establishing clear boundaries between her activism and personal life. This includes designated "off" times where she disconnects from social media and activism-related tasks, allowing her to recharge.

- **Mindfulness Practices:** Engaging in mindfulness practices such as meditation, yoga, or simply taking walks in nature has become a cornerstone of Sally's self-care routine. Research indicates that mindfulness can significantly reduce stress and improve emotional regulation, which is crucial for activists facing constant challenges.

- **Peer Support:** Sally actively participates in peer support groups for LGBTQ activists. Sharing experiences and coping strategies with others who understand the unique pressures of activism fosters a sense of community and reduces feelings of isolation.

• **Engaging in Hobbies:** Pursuing personal interests outside of activism, such as painting or reading, helps Sally maintain a sense of identity beyond her role as an activist. Engaging in creative outlets can serve as a therapeutic escape from the pressures of her work.

## The Importance of Reflection and Adaptation

Another vital aspect of balancing activism and self-care is the practice of reflection. Sally regularly assesses her emotional and physical state, allowing her to identify signs of burnout early. This proactive approach enables her to adapt her strategies as needed, ensuring that she remains effective in her advocacy without sacrificing her well-being.

As Sally often reflects, "You can't pour from an empty cup." This metaphor encapsulates the idea that self-care is not a luxury but a necessity for sustaining long-term activism. By prioritizing her health, she is better equipped to advocate for others, embodying the very principles she fights for.

## Conclusion

In conclusion, balancing activism and self-care is an ongoing journey that requires intentionality and commitment. For Sally Rugg, integrating self-care practices into her activism has not only enhanced her personal well-being but has also amplified her effectiveness as a leader in the LGBTQ rights movement. As she continues to inspire others, her journey serves as a reminder that caring for oneself is an essential part of the fight for justice. Activists must recognize that their voices are stronger when they are grounded in well-being, making the pursuit of self-care a vital component of any advocacy strategy.

## Looking towards the future

As Sally Rugg reflects on her journey as an activist, she recognizes that the fight for LGBTQ rights is far from over. The future is a canvas yet to be painted, and it requires both vision and action to ensure that the progress made is not only sustained but also expanded. The landscape of activism is ever-evolving, and with it comes new challenges and opportunities that demand innovative approaches and unwavering commitment.

## Theoretical Frameworks for Future Activism

Looking ahead, it is essential to ground future activism in robust theoretical frameworks that address the complexities of identity and intersectionality. Theories such as *Critical Race Theory* (CRT) and *Queer Theory* provide vital lenses through which to examine the multifaceted nature of oppression and privilege. These frameworks encourage activists to consider how race, gender, sexuality, and socioeconomic status intersect to shape individual experiences and systemic inequalities.

For instance, CRT emphasizes the importance of understanding how laws and policies can perpetuate racial inequalities, which can also be applied to LGBTQ issues. By recognizing that LGBTQ individuals of color often face compounded discrimination, activists can tailor their strategies to address these unique challenges. This intersectional approach is crucial for creating inclusive movements that uplift all members of the LGBTQ community.

## Anticipating Challenges

The future of LGBTQ activism will inevitably encounter challenges that require resilience and adaptability. One pressing issue is the backlash against LGBTQ rights, which has been evident in various regions around the globe. For example, recent legislative efforts in some U.S. states aimed at restricting transgender rights have sparked widespread protests and mobilization efforts. Activists must prepare for similar pushbacks in other regions, including Australia, where conservative political factions may seek to roll back hard-won rights.

Moreover, the rise of misinformation and hate speech, particularly on social media platforms, presents a formidable challenge. Activists must develop strategies to combat these narratives effectively. This includes not only countering misinformation with factual information but also fostering a culture of empathy and understanding within broader society. Engaging in dialogue, storytelling, and community-building can help bridge divides and reduce hostility.

## Innovative Strategies for Engagement

To navigate these challenges, Sally Rugg emphasizes the need for innovative strategies that leverage technology and grassroots organizing. Social media has proven to be a powerful tool for mobilization and awareness, but it must be used thoughtfully. Future activism should focus on creating safe online spaces where individuals can share their stories and connect with others. This can involve utilizing platforms like Instagram and TikTok to amplify diverse voices and experiences within the LGBTQ community.

In addition to digital engagement, grassroots organizing remains a cornerstone of effective activism. Building coalitions with other marginalized groups can strengthen movements and create a united front against discrimination. For example, partnerships with feminist organizations, racial justice groups, and disability rights advocates can enhance the visibility and impact of LGBTQ issues. By working together, these coalitions can address the systemic nature of oppression and advocate for comprehensive policy changes.

## Empowering Future Generations

Central to looking towards the future is the empowerment of young activists. Sally Rugg recognizes the importance of mentorship and education in fostering the next generation of leaders. By establishing programs that connect experienced activists with youth, knowledge and skills can be passed down effectively. Workshops, training sessions, and speaking engagements in schools and universities can inspire young people to take action and advocate for their rights and the rights of others.

Furthermore, creating platforms for young LGBTQ voices to be heard is vital. Initiatives that highlight the experiences and perspectives of LGBTQ youth can help shape the narrative around LGBTQ rights and influence policy decisions. For example, youth-led campaigns and advocacy efforts can draw attention to issues such as mental health, bullying, and access to education, ensuring that the needs of younger generations are prioritized.

## A Vision for an Inclusive Future

Ultimately, looking towards the future means envisioning an inclusive society where LGBTQ individuals can thrive without fear of discrimination or violence. This vision requires collective action and a commitment to social justice that transcends individual identities. By fostering a culture of acceptance, understanding, and love, activists can create a world where diversity is celebrated, and all individuals can live authentically.

In conclusion, as Sally Rugg looks towards the future, she is filled with hope and determination. The road ahead may be fraught with challenges, but with a solid theoretical foundation, innovative strategies, and a commitment to empowering future generations, the LGBTQ movement can continue to make strides toward equality and justice. The legacy of activism is not just about the battles fought but about the futures forged through resilience, solidarity, and unwavering belief in the power of love and acceptance.

# Conclusion

## Sally Rugg's impact on LGBTQ activism

### Inspiring a generation of activists

Sally Rugg's journey through the landscape of LGBTQ activism has not only marked her as a prominent figure in the movement but has also ignited a spark that has inspired countless individuals to take up the mantle of advocacy. Her story is one of resilience, determination, and a deep commitment to justice that resonates with a generation yearning for change.

At the heart of Rugg's influence lies her ability to articulate the struggles faced by the LGBTQ community in a way that is both relatable and empowering. By sharing her personal narrative—her struggles with identity, the pain of discrimination, and the triumphs of advocacy—she has created a blueprint for emerging activists. This narrative approach is supported by the theory of narrative identity, which posits that individuals construct their identities through stories, thus allowing them to connect with others who share similar experiences [?].

Rugg's speeches and public appearances often highlight the importance of community and solidarity. For instance, during her address at the Sydney Gay and Lesbian Mardi Gras, she emphasized the collective power of voices united in a common cause. This moment not only galvanized the crowd but also served as a catalyst for many to join the movement, illustrating the theory of collective efficacy, which suggests that individuals are more likely to engage in activism when they perceive their collective efforts will lead to significant change [?].

One of the most significant aspects of Rugg's impact is her focus on mentorship and empowerment of LGBTQ youth. Through initiatives such as workshops and speaking engagements at schools, she has fostered an environment where young activists can thrive. By providing them with the tools and confidence to advocate for their rights, Rugg embodies the principles of transformational leadership, which emphasizes the importance of inspiring and empowering followers to achieve their full potential [?].

Moreover, Rugg's strategic use of social media has played a crucial role in mobilizing a new generation of activists. Platforms like Instagram and Twitter have allowed her to reach a wider audience, breaking down barriers of access to information and engagement. This phenomenon aligns with the theory of networked activism, which posits that social media can amplify voices and create communities that transcend geographical limitations [?]. By leveraging these platforms, Rugg has not only shared her message but has also encouraged others to share theirs, fostering a culture of activism that is inclusive and diverse.

However, the path to activism is fraught with challenges. Many young activists face backlash, discrimination, and even threats as they step into the public sphere. Rugg has openly addressed these issues, providing a realistic portrayal of the struggles that accompany activism. Her openness about her own experiences with hate speech and personal attacks serves as a powerful reminder that resilience is key. This perspective aligns with the psychological resilience theory, which emphasizes the capacity to recover from difficulties and maintain mental health despite adversity [?].

Rugg's legacy is further solidified through her contributions to legislative victories, such as the successful campaign for marriage equality in Australia. By mobilizing a generation around this pivotal issue, she has demonstrated the tangible impact of grassroots activism. The success of this campaign serves as a case study in effective advocacy, illustrating how strategic planning, community engagement, and persistent effort can lead to meaningful change.

In conclusion, Sally Rugg's influence extends far beyond her own accomplishments; she has inspired a generation of activists to embrace their identities, advocate for their rights, and strive for a more equitable society. Her story exemplifies the power of personal narrative, community solidarity, and strategic activism in shaping the future of LGBTQ rights. As Rugg continues to lead and inspire, her legacy will undoubtedly empower future generations to carry the torch of activism forward, ensuring that the fight for equality remains vibrant and relentless.

## Shaping the narrative of LGBTQ rights in Australia

The journey of LGBTQ rights in Australia has been a complex tapestry woven with threads of struggle, resilience, and triumph. At the forefront of this evolution has been Sally Rugg, whose advocacy has played a pivotal role in shaping the narrative surrounding LGBTQ rights in the nation. This section delves into the various dimensions of this narrative, highlighting key theories, persistent problems, and significant examples that illustrate the profound impact of Rugg's activism.

## Theoretical Frameworks

To understand the shaping of LGBTQ rights narratives, we can draw on several theoretical frameworks. One such framework is **Social Movement Theory**, which posits that social movements arise in response to perceived injustices and mobilize individuals towards collective action. This theory elucidates how Rugg's activism emerged from a backdrop of systemic discrimination and societal marginalization faced by LGBTQ individuals in Australia.

Additionally, **Intersectionality** is crucial in analyzing the LGBTQ rights narrative. Coined by Kimberlé Crenshaw, this theory emphasizes the interconnectedness of social categorizations such as race, gender, and sexual orientation, which can create overlapping systems of discrimination. Rugg's advocacy has often highlighted the importance of recognizing these intersections, particularly in addressing the unique challenges faced by LGBTQ individuals from diverse backgrounds.

## Persistent Problems

Despite significant progress, numerous challenges persist in the fight for LGBTQ rights in Australia. One of the most pressing issues is the ongoing discrimination faced by LGBTQ individuals in various sectors, including employment, healthcare, and education. According to a 2021 report by the Australian Human Rights Commission, approximately 60% of LGBTQ individuals have experienced discrimination in the workplace, underscoring the need for continued advocacy.

Moreover, the mental health crisis within the LGBTQ community remains a critical concern. Studies indicate that LGBTQ youth are significantly more likely to experience mental health issues, including depression and anxiety, compared to their heterosexual peers. Rugg's focus on mental health advocacy has been instrumental in bringing these issues to the forefront of public discourse, emphasizing the need for comprehensive support systems.

## Key Examples of Narrative Shaping

Rugg's activism has been characterized by several landmark moments that have contributed to reshaping the narrative of LGBTQ rights in Australia. One such moment was her involvement in the **Marriage Equality Campaign**, which culminated in the legalization of same-sex marriage in December 2017. Rugg's tireless efforts in mobilizing public support and engaging with policymakers were instrumental in shifting societal attitudes towards marriage equality.

The campaign was not merely about legal recognition; it represented a broader fight for dignity and respect. Rugg utilized various platforms—social media, public speeches, and community engagement—to humanize the issue, sharing personal stories that resonated with the Australian public. This approach exemplified the power of narrative in activism, illustrating how personal experiences can catalyze collective change.

Another significant aspect of Rugg's impact is her role in enhancing the visibility of LGBTQ issues in mainstream media. Through her appearances on television and radio, Rugg has challenged stereotypes and misconceptions about the LGBTQ community, fostering a more nuanced understanding among the general public. For instance, her participation in high-profile interviews has often centered around the lived experiences of LGBTQ individuals, effectively humanizing the struggles faced by the community.

## Conclusion

In conclusion, Sally Rugg's activism has been instrumental in shaping the narrative of LGBTQ rights in Australia. By leveraging theoretical frameworks such as Social Movement Theory and Intersectionality, Rugg has addressed persistent problems within the community while advocating for systemic change. Her involvement in key campaigns, particularly the Marriage Equality Campaign, alongside her efforts to enhance media representation, has significantly influenced public perception and policy. As Australia continues to navigate the complexities of LGBTQ rights, Rugg's legacy serves as a beacon of hope and a reminder of the power of narrative in driving social change.

## A force for change and progress

Sally Rugg has emerged as a formidable force in the landscape of LGBTQ activism, fundamentally reshaping the dialogue surrounding rights and representation. Her journey exemplifies the intersection of personal experience and systemic change, showcasing how individual narratives can catalyze broader societal transformation.

At the core of Rugg's activism lies the theory of **social change**, which posits that collective action can lead to significant shifts in societal norms and values. As articulated by theorists such as Charles Tilly, social movements are often the result of sustained efforts by marginalized groups to challenge existing power structures.

Rugg's work aligns with this theory, as she has mobilized communities, engaged in strategic advocacy, and utilized media platforms to amplify LGBTQ voices.

## Theoretical Frameworks

Rugg's activism can be analyzed through the lens of **intersectionality**, a term coined by Kimberlé Crenshaw. This framework emphasizes the interconnected nature of social categorizations such as race, class, and gender, which create overlapping systems of discrimination and disadvantage. Rugg has consistently highlighted the importance of intersectionality in her advocacy, recognizing that LGBTQ rights cannot be viewed in isolation from issues such as racial inequality, economic disparity, and gender identity. This holistic approach has allowed her to build coalitions across various movements, fostering solidarity among diverse groups.

Moreover, Rugg's strategies reflect the principles of **community organizing**, a method that emphasizes grassroots mobilization and empowerment. By creating spaces for dialogue and collaboration, she has enabled individuals within the LGBTQ community to articulate their needs and advocate for their rights. This approach not only empowers individuals but also strengthens the collective voice of the community, making it a powerful force for change.

## Challenges and Obstacles

Despite her successes, Rugg's journey has not been without challenges. The LGBTQ rights movement in Australia has faced significant obstacles, including entrenched homophobia, legislative hurdles, and societal resistance to change. For instance, the fight for marriage equality was fraught with opposition, as conservative factions mobilized to maintain the status quo. Rugg's response to these challenges exemplifies her resilience and determination.

In 2017, during the national postal survey on marriage equality, Rugg played a pivotal role in organizing campaigns that encouraged public participation. Her efforts were instrumental in countering misinformation and galvanizing support for the "Yes" campaign. The survey ultimately resulted in a landmark victory for LGBTQ rights in Australia, with over 61% of voters supporting marriage equality. This achievement not only validated the experiences of countless individuals but also signaled a shift in societal attitudes toward LGBTQ relationships.

## Examples of Progress

Rugg's influence extends beyond marriage equality. She has been a vocal advocate for comprehensive anti-discrimination laws, emphasizing the need for protections that encompass not only sexual orientation but also gender identity and expression. Her work with various organizations has contributed to the introduction of policies that safeguard LGBTQ individuals from discrimination in employment, housing, and healthcare.

One notable example of Rugg's impact is her involvement in the campaign for the **Safe Schools Program**, an initiative aimed at creating inclusive educational environments for LGBTQ students. Despite facing significant backlash from conservative groups, Rugg's advocacy helped to ensure that the program was implemented in schools across Australia, providing vital resources and support for LGBTQ youth.

## Sustaining Momentum

To sustain momentum for progress, Rugg emphasizes the importance of **youth engagement**. She recognizes that empowering the next generation of activists is crucial for the longevity of the movement. Through mentorship programs and educational initiatives, Rugg has worked to cultivate leadership skills among young LGBTQ individuals, ensuring that they have the tools necessary to advocate for their rights.

Additionally, Rugg's commitment to intersectionality has fostered a more inclusive movement, encouraging the participation of marginalized voices within the LGBTQ community. By centering the experiences of individuals from diverse backgrounds, she has expanded the scope of activism, making it more representative and effective.

In conclusion, Sally Rugg's role as a force for change and progress within the LGBTQ rights movement is characterized by her unwavering commitment to advocacy, intersectionality, and community empowerment. Her ability to navigate challenges, mobilize support, and inspire others has not only transformed the landscape of LGBTQ rights in Australia but has also set a precedent for future activism. As the movement continues to evolve, Rugg's legacy will undoubtedly serve as a guiding light for generations to come, reminding us that change is possible when we stand together in solidarity.

$$\text{Change} = \text{Advocacy} + \text{Community Empowerment} + \text{Intersectionality} \quad (19)$$

## Sally Rugg: The legacy continues

Sally Rugg's journey as an LGBTQ activist transcends the confines of her immediate achievements; it embodies a legacy that continues to inspire and galvanize future generations. Her work has not only altered the landscape of LGBTQ rights in Australia but has also contributed to a global dialogue about equality, acceptance, and the ongoing fight against discrimination. This legacy is built on several foundational pillars: advocacy, empowerment, and resilience.

### Advocacy for Equality

Rugg's advocacy has been instrumental in shaping policies that promote equality. Her co-founding of the Marriage Equality Campaign exemplifies a strategic approach to activism, where grassroots mobilization meets legislative pressure. The campaign's success in achieving marriage equality in Australia stands as a testament to her unyielding commitment to justice.

Theoretical frameworks such as the *Social Movement Theory* can be applied to analyze her impact. According to Charles Tilly's framework, social movements succeed when they can mobilize resources, create a collective identity, and engage in political opportunities. Rugg's ability to harness public sentiment and mobilize supporters through social media platforms exemplifies this theory in action.

$$\text{Success} = f(\text{Mobilization, Resource Availability, Political Opportunity}) \quad (20)$$

Where: - *Mobilization* refers to the ability to rally supporters. - *Resource Availability* encompasses funding, manpower, and organizational support. - *Political Opportunity* involves favorable political climates for advocacy.

Rugg's strategic navigation of these elements has not only led to legislative victories but also fostered a sense of community among LGBTQ individuals and allies.

### Empowerment of Future Generations

A significant aspect of Rugg's legacy is her dedication to empowering LGBTQ youth. Through mentoring programs and educational initiatives, she has created pathways for young activists to find their voice and engage in advocacy. By emphasizing the importance of intersectionality, Rugg has broadened the scope of activism to include diverse identities within the LGBTQ spectrum, addressing issues that impact marginalized groups.

For instance, her involvement in speaking engagements at schools and universities has allowed her to connect with young people, encouraging them to share their stories and experiences. This empowerment is crucial, as research indicates that youth who feel supported in their identities are more likely to engage in civic activities and advocacy.

$$\text{Youth Empowerment} \propto \text{Support} \times \text{Engagement} \qquad (21)$$

Where: - *Support* reflects the encouragement and resources provided to youth. - *Engagement* denotes active participation in community and advocacy efforts.

Rugg's efforts have not only uplifted individual voices but have also contributed to a collective narrative that emphasizes the importance of diversity and inclusion within the LGBTQ movement.

## Resilience in the Face of Adversity

The challenges Rugg faced—ranging from public scrutiny to personal attacks—underscore a broader narrative of resilience within the LGBTQ community. Her ability to confront hate speech and backlash with grace and determination serves as an inspiration to many. The psychological resilience she embodies can be analyzed through the lens of *Resilience Theory*, which posits that individuals can thrive despite adversity through supportive relationships and adaptive coping strategies.

Rugg's public stance against discrimination and her commitment to self-care highlight the importance of mental health in activism. By openly discussing her struggles, she normalizes the conversation around mental health within the LGBTQ community, encouraging others to seek help and support.

## Looking Ahead

As we reflect on Sally Rugg's legacy, it is essential to recognize that the fight for LGBTQ rights is far from over. The ongoing challenges faced by transgender individuals, particularly regarding healthcare access and legal recognition, require sustained advocacy. Rugg's legacy serves as a rallying cry for continued activism, reminding us that progress is a collective endeavor.

In conclusion, Sally Rugg's impact on LGBTQ activism is profound and multifaceted. Her advocacy has reshaped policies, empowered youth, and exemplified resilience in the face of adversity. As we move forward, her legacy will undoubtedly continue to inspire and mobilize future generations to fight for equality and justice, ensuring that the narrative of LGBTQ rights remains vibrant and dynamic.

$$Legacy = Advocacy + Empowerment + Resilience \qquad (22)$$

# Index